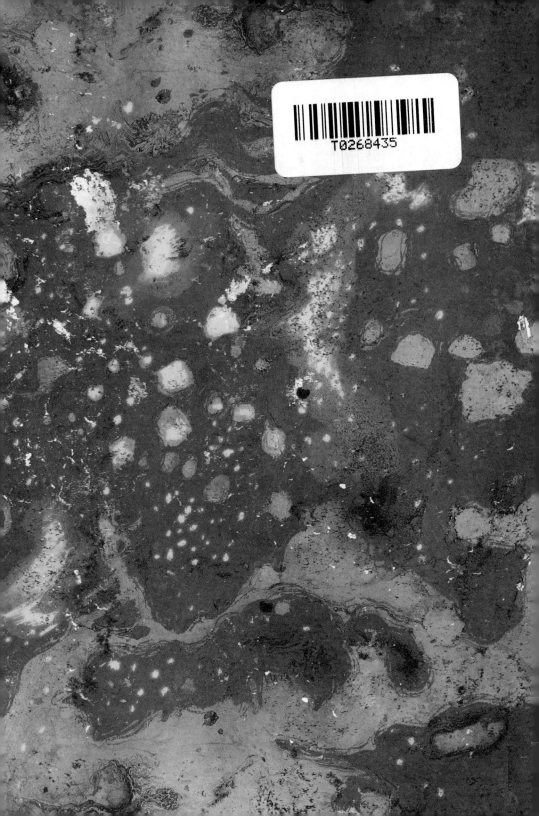

the Night School for Young Mystics

Five Fabulous Field Trips
into Moonlight & Magic

MAIA TOLL

illustrated by **KHOA LE**

RP|KIDS
PHILADELPHIA

Running Press Kids
Hachette Book Group
1290 Avenue of the Americas, New York, NY 10104
www.runningpress.com/rpkids
@runningpresskids

Distributed in the United Kingdom by Little, Brown Book Group UK,
Carmelite House, 50 Victoria Embankment, London, EC4Y 0DZ

Printed in China

First Edition: August 2024

Published by Running Press Kids, an imprint of Hachette Book Group, Inc.
The Running Press Kids name and logo are trademarks of Hachette Book Group, Inc.

The Hachette Speakers Bureau provides a wide range of authors
for speaking events. To find out more, go to www.hachettespeakersbureau.com
or email HachetteSpeakers@hbgusa.com.

Running Press books may be purchased in bulk for business, educational,
or promotional use. For more information, please contact your local bookseller or
the Hachette Book Group Special Markets Department at Special.Markets@hbgusa.com.

The publisher is not responsible for websites
(or their content) that are not owned by the publisher.

Print book cover and interior design by Frances J. Soo Ping Chow.
Icons copyright © Getty Images/RLT_Images

Library of Congress Control Number: 2023022185

ISBNs: 978-0-7624-8610-6 (hardcover), 978-0-7624-8612-0 (ebook)

1010

10 9 8 7 6 5 4 3 2 1

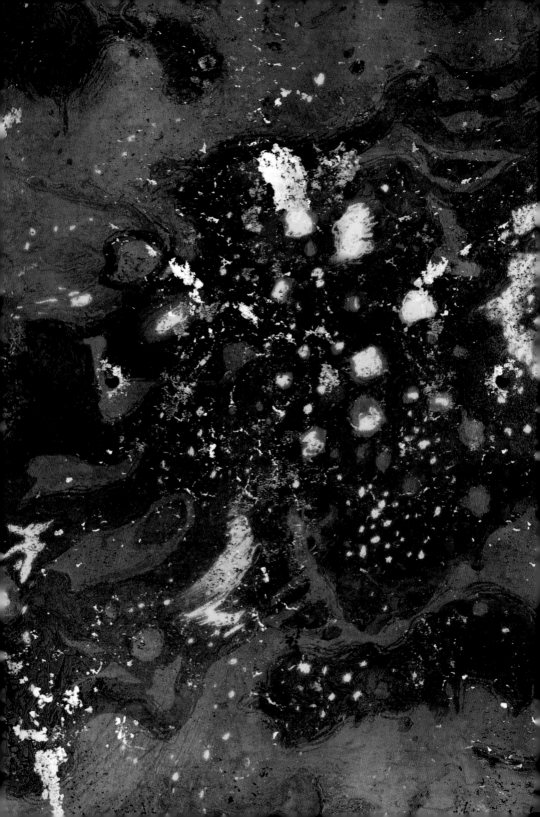

CONTENTS

WELCOME TO THE
NIGHT SCHOOL!
LETTER OF ACCEPTANCE

Congratulations, Firefly, you're in!

You've been chosen, through your own rigorous self-examination, to join the Night School's esteemed program for the study of magic and mysticism. Holding this book and reading this letter is the first step in delving into the mysterious depths both within you and in the Universe around you.

You already have everything you need to be successful at the Night School:

- ✳ a sense of adventure
- ✳ a willingness to question your own thoughts and beliefs
- ✳ a deep desire to think—not in a straight line, but in circles and spirals and shooting stars (How do you think in shooting stars? Stay tuned!)

At the Night School, we believe magic should be experienced. Through a series of "field trips," you'll explore the unseen underbelly of life (because everyone who owns a dog knows that the underbelly is where the magic is!) and ponder questions rarely thought of by the light of day. Pondering and questioning will lead you closer to *your* truths, which are the most important truths of all.

That's right, Firefly, you have your very own truths. At the Night School, you'll discover the shape of them and how they can help you to create your very own magical life.

So you can get to know me, I've included my CV (CV is an abbreviation for *curriculum vitae*. That's Latin. It means *the course of one's life*. My CV is a short course on *my* life, which I do hope you'll enjoy! I've tried, as I do in all things, to make it interesting for both of us.) Please also see the attached school mantra, supply list, and schedule.

Welcome to the Night School!

Yours in starlight,

Bea Marlowe

Head teacher, the Night School

HEAD TEACHER BEA MARLOWE'S
CURRICULUM VITAE

Hi there, Firefly! I'm Beatrice Marlowe. That's Ms. Marlowe to you, Bea to my friends. I'm very honored to be the head teacher at the Night School.

The above portrait was done by the fabulous Khoa Le. I met her in Paris while waiting in line at my favorite bakery. We bonded over a love of baguettes (the long breads that are crunchy on the outside and deliciously soft in the middle), and then, voilà!, before I'd given it half a thought, I was in her studio posing for a portrait. Sometimes friendships happen like that, mais oui?

But what's more important is why I was in Paris in the first place: I was there to take a cooking class.

Cooking? you say. *What's so mystical about cooking?*

Let me explain:

I learned about the Mysteries from my father, who learned from my grandmother, and so on and so on, back and back and back to a group of poets, scientists, and philosophers dubbed the School of the Night. Doesn't that sound fascinatingly mysterious? The School of the Night was formed in England in the 1500s. The members of the school met in secret to talk about **philosophy**. And while philosophy is very interesting stuff to think about, it isn't particularly useful on a daily basis. My dad thought that magic should be more than just theory and fluff: It should inform your everyday life. And what could be more daily life than whipping up a delicious dinner? Cooking is its own bit of magic: It uses all the building blocks of the Universe!

What do I mean by that?

Let's pause for a lesson. I'm always pausing for lessons. I find them quite charming, and one should always take a moment to examine them when they cross your path!

A Quick Lesson on the Elements

Back in the early days, when humans were trying to figure out how life on Earth worked, there were a bunch of philosophers who decided to find the one building block that was used to create everything in the Universe. It turns out, this was a tough task! For many years, the philosophers thought, drew diagrams on napkins, paced in circles, and thought some more. After all this thinking, they decided there was not *one* building block of the Universe, but instead that everything was made from *four* building blocks, which they called *the elements*: Earth, Air, Water, and Fire.

Fast-forward a few thousand years. Scientists have continued to ask these very same questions. Modern science teaches that Earth, Air, Water, and Fire are *not* the primary building blocks of the Universe. Instead, there are atoms and their component parts. But our Night-brains hardly seem to notice this newish-knowledge: Our connection with the original four elements remains.

I think, Firefly, that's because the four elements are symbols that help us better understand ourselves and the world around us. They give us a way of thinking about not just physical things, but also emotions and thoughts. Take a look for yourself!

Earth

Your derriere is most likely resting on something made from the Earth element. Earth is stable, making it a fine element for furniture as well as for boulders and tree stumps. Material things—like humans, chairs, and carrots—are made of Earth and will eventually return to Earth, where microbes in the soil will break down and compost the material. The breaking down of these materials allows them to be reused, becoming building blocks for something new.

There are some emotions that feel just as stable as a chair: the feeling of a good, solid friendship or the happiness you feel when you watch the sunrise. These feelings are earthy.

Air

Air used to be called wind. When the wind blows, change is coming! The wind can blow in a blizzard or a summer storm. It can topple trees and lawn chairs. Air's turnabouts can be quick, often happening at the speed of thought (as in: *I changed my mind! No cookies for that midnight snack; I think I'd prefer pie . . . or spaghetti. Hmmm . . .*).

Start with your own breath—inhale, exhale. That's Air. If you listen, you can hear it in the quiet *whoosh* of the heated or air-conditioned drafts passing through the vents in your home or in the wind rustling the Night branches.

Because of its ability to move and change, Air reflects our brain's gymnastics as it does its light-speed thinking. So, we use Air as a symbol for thoughts and thinking as well as for talking, singing, teaching, and other things you do with your voice (because your vocal cords run on Air, Firefly!).

Water

At its most basic level, Water is the stuff in the glass or mug from which you're drinking. It doesn't matter what kind of liquid is in the cup, Firefly: If it's a liquid, it falls under the Water element. Remember, none of this is written in stone (which, by the way, would be the Earth element). And it can get a little confusing when we're talking about H_2O because Water is what we call *mutable*: That means it can move from solid (ice) to liquid (water) to air (vapor). So, Water is liquid . . . except when it's not. Because of this, Water represents what is mutable and changeable within us: our emotions (which gives you a clue about the healthiest emotional state. In the body, we see it in our tears, so sadness and grief are also the domain of water.

Fire

Fire was the one element that didn't come right to our hand. The earliest humanoid gasped in a first breath of Air, sat on the Earth to rest, and cupped their hands to sip from the Water in a stream. But Fire was distant: It radiated down from the sun and flashed across the Night sky as lightning and shooting stars. It was a thing of the heavens.

So, how did people master this cosmic element?

Stories vary (and all we have are stories, Firefly: The taming of Fire took place long before there was written record. In fact, the first evidence of Fire, based on identifying and dating charcoal residue, took place in what geologists call *deep time*—the stretch of the Earth's history before humans inhabited it). The Greeks credit a guy named Prometheus with stealing Fire from the gods. The Tagish peoples of Canada tell the tale of Crow bringing Fire. And in Polynesian mythology, Fire was stolen from the Fire goddess Mahuika. In all these stories, Fire is brought down from the celestial region of the sky.

And, most likely, that's what happened: A lightning strike caused a small Fire that our deep time ancestors captured and nurtured, carrying it from campfire to campfire. In a literal flash, Fire-keeping became the most important position in any hunter/gatherer group.

Fire provided more than a warm place to sleep and protection from other animals (who still saw Fire and thought, *RUN!*). Fire gave these early humanoids a place to roast marshmallows and toast s'mores. Since it's well known that the nutritional value of marshmallows and graham crackers can only be unlocked when cooked, mastering the Fire element for cooking meant that food suddenly had a higher nutritional value. (Kidding aside, Firefly, when you cook food, you are beginning to break down the fibers and proteins, essentially pre-digesting it, so that by the time you put the food inside your stomach, there's less work to do in order to get the nutritional components.) A study out of the Institute of Biomedical Sciences at the Federal University of Rio de Janeiro in Brazil was able to match the time lines for cooking food with the increased brain size of our ancestors.

You can see from Fire's prehistoric beginnings why it became the element associated with warmth and passion. And these earliest Fire users had to be extremely creative to move from barbecue to brûlée. The words for *cook* and *magic* were actually the same in Ancient Greek—isn't that fascinating, Firefly? The cook was the magician who doubled our brain-span, thus creating mental space to dream up roller derbies, ramen noodles, and rock and roll. I'm sure you can now see why I spent time studying cooking in Paris, which is what I was mentioning before I took us on this quick side trip!

Wasn't that a fun little excursion, Firefly? Lessons are so adorable. I really do hope another crosses our path!

Now, where were we before I sidetracked us?

Oh, yes: When not learning from my father, I spent time studying with the Ancient Order of **Astrologers** and also at the Guild of Modern **Alchemy**. After returning from a year in Wales learning from a family of witches (alas, field trips to visit them have been canceled since the rather unfortunate **cauldron** incident), I did a six-month stint with the secret sect of the **Pythian** Priestesses to learn the art of divination (*divination* means reading the future, Firefly). I've arranged a field trip there, so you will get to learn directly from these divine ladies!

There's a lot that's "secret" in the mystical world. I founded the Night School to share these secrets and mysteries, because we all need a bit of magic in our lives.

Now that I've introduced myself, it's time to sip the Moon Juice! Let's begin with the Night School **mantra**. You'll want to memorize this before your first field trip.

THE NIGHT SCHOOL MANTRA

Our school's mantra contains the most important lesson you will learn here, Firefly. These lessons stitch together all the learning to come. This is the foundation for everything that will follow in your Night School studies. You'll want to be sure to memorize it as soon as possible. To help, write it out, tape it to your bathroom mirror, and read it every morning and evening while you brush your teeth until you can recite it with your eyes closed.

Ready?

Magic is everywhere.
To see it and the effects it has on your life,
 change the way you look at the world.
To harness it,
 change the way you work with
  the energies around you.
To know it,
 change the way you think.
To live it,
 remember the lessons of the Night
  as you go about your day.

This mantra is your starting point. If you get stuck as you work through your lessons, return to these words so you can remember how to let magic into your mind and your life.

If you hit a roadblock in your studies, it probably means that you have reverted to previous thought patterns. Old thought forms are like a pair of well-worn pajamas: They're so comfortable they're hard to get rid of, even when they're full of holes. Use the Night School mantra to, quite literally, change your mind. (Minds are amazingly squishy and truly don't mind being changed!)

Still, go easy on yourself. Most likely you grew up in a daylight culture, and your brain is used to understanding the world based on strict daylight logic. But the Night is vast and mysterious. The Night exists to balance the day, and so, to balance yourself, you must give space to the darkness. Never fear: Your new thought forms will become soft and soothing once you break them in.

On that note, let's prepare to step into the Night!

THE NIGHT SCHOOL
SUPPLY LIST

I've compiled a list of the supplies you'll need so you can complete your studies at the Night School. You won't need every item for every field trip, so be sure to consult each trip's packing list before you go!

Don't panic if there are items listed here that you don't have at home! There's no need to do extensive shopping. Following the list below, I have studies that go over each item in detail, including substitutions and home-made versions (which often work just as well as anything bought from a store).

SUPPLIES FOR
ALL NIGHT SCHOOL STUDIES

* a notebook
* a flashlight
* a window, deck, porch, front stoop, sit spot, or meadow
* a pocket compass
* a rattle

* a pendulum
* a magazine with lots of pictures
* a pocket full of pebbles or a bowl of dried beans
* salt

A Notebook

Your most important supply is your notebook! There are many types of books you can write in: a standard notebook with lines or a sketchbook without lines; a book that's spiral-bound or has a stitched spine; a small journal that fits in your pocket or a big notebook that sits across your knees. Your notebook (also called a *field journal*) should be inviting; it should make you want to write or doodle or draw inside it. If it doesn't feel friendly, then it's not the right notebook for you.

A Flashlight

Sometimes I'll ask you to turn out the lights or step outside into the Night. Even when the goal is to experience the darkness, you'll want something to light your way—there's no need to twist an ankle. A phone with a light or a sturdy flashlight will do the trick. Candles are magical, but walking around with an open flame is a fabulous way to start a fire. Your great-great-great-grandmother put her candle inside a sturdy glass lantern for a reason!

A Window, Deck, Porch, Front Stoop,
Sit Spot, or Meadow

Basically, what you are looking for is a place where you can feel the vastness of the Night sky and let your mind drift. So pick your spot! It doesn't matter where your place is—what matters is that you feel safe and can turn off any electric lights in your immediate vicinity. Trust me, Firefly, the Night has a different energy without those buzzy little lights. I want you to have a chance to experience this.

Remember: the Night is not simply the stretch of time after the sun goes down. The Night is the shadows, the silence, and the stars. The Night is lit differently than the day, so everything looks a little distorted (it's important to note that your eyes depend on light, Firefly, so when you change the quality of the light, you change what you see). Find a place where you can leave the electric lights behind and let your eyes and mind adjust to a world that is softer and less defined—a world with mysteries in every shadow. This is the Night we are stepping into.

Note: Talk to an adult about your chosen spot. It's important for someone to know where you are when you're outside in the dark. Depending on where you live, the very best spot might be sitting inside in front of an open window with the lights turned off in the room behind you.

A Pocket Compass

You know that the sun rises in the east and sets in the west, right, Firefly? But how do you determine direction when the sun is sleeping? Some people learn to navigate by the stars, but it's also helpful to have a compass to guide your way. You'll learn to use a compass in more depth during field trip #1!

Compasses also serve a secondary purpose: The presence of a compass is the best way to identify fellow Night School students. If you see something that looks like a **watch fob** hanging from someone's pocket, suspect another student is in your midst. If you're passing this person on the street or standing next to them in line at the cafeteria, the proper protocol is to half smile with the right side of your mouth and to nod your head in greeting. Please do not talk, wink, or gush. (And for goodness' sake, do not say the words *the Night School*.)

Please acquire a pocket compass as soon as possible. Begin by asking your family if anyone has one that you can use. Be sure to check with your older relatives to see if they have one tucked away (my grandpa had three stashed in his sock drawer!). If there are none available, you can find them for sale online or at a sporting goods store. A tiny keychain compass is just fine—no need to get fancy! (Or, if you like science or are crafty, you may want to make your own. Go online with a parent's permission and look up "homemade compass.")

A Rattle

Or, I should say, something that rattles. It can be an actual rattle such as a baby might use, a maraca from your musical instrument collection, or even an egg shaker. You can also make one yourself. I like to simply put something hard and dry—like dried beans, rice, or paper clips—into a mason jar!

A Pendulum

A pendulum is a tool for dowsing. You'll learn all about dowsing when we study divination, Firefly! It's easy to make your own pendulum at home. Simply tie an old key or ring to a string.

A Magazine with Lots of Pictures

You'll be cutting out pictures for various uses! My favorite magazines for this purpose are travel magazines or *National Geographic* because these types of magazines have *so* many different types of photographs. But you might prefer a magazine with animal pictures or images of houses. The type of magazine doesn't matter, so long as it has lots of pictures to choose from.

Sometimes libraries give away old magazines once a newer issue comes out. Ask your local librarian if there are any magazines available for you to use as an art project. Check with your friends to see if they have magazines in their recycling pile at home.

Another option is to print images off the internet. But this will use a lot of paper, so the more environmentally friendly choice is to use a magazine that someone was getting rid of.

A Pocket Full of Pebbles or a Bowl of Dried Beans

You'll be using these in your final field trip, Firefly. The idea is to have a handful of *something*: pebbles, dried peas or beans, or macaroni. The *something* should be small and not fragile. Use what you have on hand!

Salt

In the world of the Night, salt is a symbol as much as a mineral. It's the blood in your veins and your connection to your ancestors. It's the waters of the world and the fish that swim in their depths. The world is full of salt, and every mystic who has ever lived has used it at one point or another.

Salt is one of the oldest tools of the magical trade. There's pink, there's gray, there's Celtic, and there's Dead Sea. It's all the same, and yet, it's all different. Choose whatever appeals most to start with. I'm a huge fan of using whatever's in your cupboard. Over time you can compare, contrast, and become a connoisseur of all different kinds of salts.

That's it, Firefly! Gather what you need either from home or from a store or online (ask an adult for help!). And remember your items don't have to be gorgeous or gilded. They just have to make your hands tingle in anticipation of what you are about to learn.

YOUR NIGHT SCHOOL
SCHEDULE

FIELD TRIP #1:

Your Night Spot: Get to Know the Night

FIELD TRIP #2:

Ms. Marlowe's Magical Library:
Study the Philosophy of Magic

FIELD TRIP #3:

The Mystery School of YOU:
Meet the Mystic Within

FIELD TRIP #4:

The World Headquarters of Witchery Marketing, LLC:
Cast a Spell!

FIELD TRIP #5:

The Secret Sect of Pythian Priestesses:
Divine the Path of the Oracle

FIELD TRIPS:
WHAT TO EXPECT

The Night School is organized around what I call "field trips." Five of them to be precise.

The bulk of these trips are, by necessity, journeys of the mind. You'll go there and back in your own head. The exception is the very first field trip, where I'll ask you to find a safe and satisfying way to experience the actual Night.

While you don't need to step out the door for our other field trips, please note that we depart together, as a group, just as the first star appears in the Night sky. So as you read your way through each field trip, know that around the world other Night School students are embarking on the same journey.

📖 Before each trip, you'll get a packing list. Be sure to have the necessary supplies on hand!

We'll be traveling together, but after we get to our destination, you'll have individual fieldwork to do. Different trips will have different assignments, but keep your eyes out for icons like this:

👁	Observe.	Sometimes we learn a lot just from noticing!
💡	Think.	On infinite interesting questions.
✏️	Write.	Just a wee assignment in your journal!
🎨	Create.	Get your hands dirty!

Occasionally a Night School student will say, "But, Ms. Marlowe! I don't want to do the assignments. Can't I just come on the field trips?"

Of course you can just join the field trips. But I would caution against this approach. True learning—the kind that settles into your bones and belly—comes from *doing, experiencing,* and *experimenting* and not merely thinking about doing, experiencing, and experimenting!

You are here to learn about magic and mysticism. Wouldn't it be sad to simply hear me discussing fabulous things while never giving yourself the opportunity to experience the magic for yourself?

Think on that while you pack your backpack because we are about to leave on our first trip!

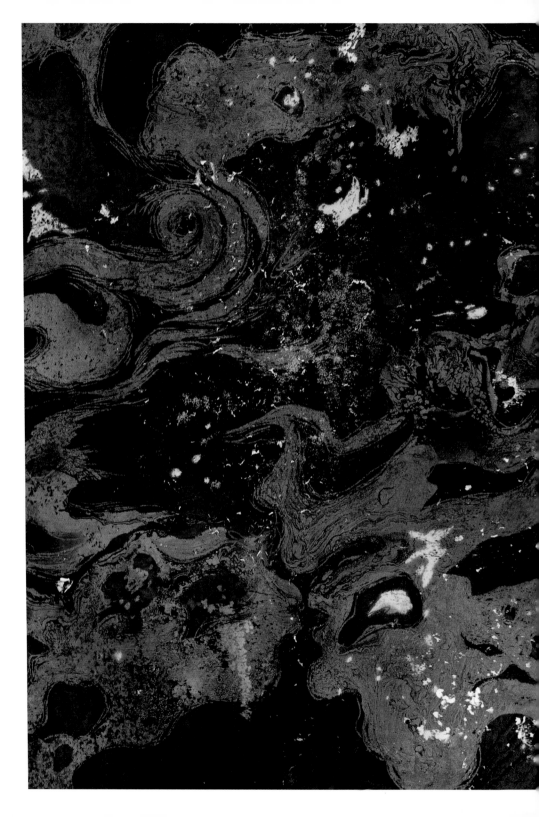

your
NIGHT
SCHOOL
Field Trips

field trip NO.1

YOUR NIGHT SPOT: GET TO KNOW THE NIGHT

YOU'LL NEED:

* a flashlight
* a compass
* your notebook

* photos from a magazine or images printed from the internet

Welcome to your first Night School field trip, Firefly!

Tonight, we'll be staying close to home (your home, that is!). Let's get comfortable with the Night and how darkness encourages you to use your senses differently than you do during daylight hours.

The Night is not only the time when the sky is dark; it's also a **metaphor** for thoughts and ideas that are sometimes hidden or for secrets you share only with yourself. Oftentimes we think that if other people knew our thoughts, they might call us silly or weird. The Night School is a place where it's safe to explore fantastical ideas and the magic that often flows in their wake.

Speaking of fantastical ideas, your future Night School trips will be made through a process called **visualization**. Don't worry, I'll walk you through it when the time comes! It's not difficult and, unlike a long car ride, will not cause motion sickness. But you will need to become very familiar with your Night Spot so you can make the return trip. I want to be sure you can always find your way home again! We'll work on this tonight.

Ready?

LET'S STEP INTO THE NIGHT

Is it dark out yet? Has the first star appeared in the sky? If so, it's time for our field trip to begin!

When the light of the sun is removed, what remains? Are the trees in your yard outlined in silver? Is your garden made of moonbeams? Are cars racing down the roads like shooting stars? Let your mind go gooey. Letting magic in is sometimes as simple as saying what the world *seems* like to you, even if you know that what you're seeing and feeling isn't literally true.

For example, every morning, right after I wake up but before I put on my glasses, I head to the kitchen to make a pot of tea. After I've scooped the Assam into the pot, I look out the window while waiting for the water to boil. (*Assam* is a variety of tea—*Camillia sinensis*—that grows in India. The scientific name of a plant is always given in Latin. And, yes, tea comes from the leaves of a plant, Firefly. But I digress!)

While waiting for the water to boil, I peer through the window, and there, right near the small laurel tree, sleeps a small black bear. She's always there, resting in my yard.

"Good morning, Ms. Bear," I murmur as I wait for my tea to steep.

Once I've drunk my tea, I go to the bedroom and get dressed. When I next come into the kitchen, I have on my glasses. The bear is gone, and in her place sits a large boulder.

My logical brain says, "There's no bear, Bea. You just can't see very well without your glasses." But my magical mind knows there's a bear who greets me every morning. You are allowed to have both: a logical mind and a magical mind. Over time, they'll figure out how to get along!

So when you walk out into the Night, allow your magical mind to take the lead.

> 💡 How long is the Night where you live? The exact length of the Night will vary depending on the time of year and where you live on this ever-rotating sky sphere we call Earth. Usually, though, the Night is between eight and twelve hours of every twenty-four-hour period.
>
> Tomorrow, note what time the sun sets and also what time it rises. Count the hours and minutes in between. Do this again in six months and see if the Night has gotten longer, shorter, or stayed the same!

Your job tonight is to activate your Night Sight: the kaleidoscope of information you receive from your senses when the world is dark. Once activated, you'll be able to use your Night Sight even in the light of day, but it is far easier to step into the Mysteries of the magical world for the first time during the hours of darkness.

We'll begin tonight's field trip with getting to know the Night. Not the words *the night*, or the concept of "the night," but the actual sueded darkness of Night—the one that exists right outside your door.

Grab your coat or find your window seat. It's time to explore the Night!

To begin, search for a star so you can breathe in its light. Maybe you'll sit on your front stoop or in a chair on the porch. Perhaps you have a backyard where you can put down a blanket and lie down to watch the stars. If you can't fit your whole body outside, that's okay! Instead, open a window and shut off the lights in the room behind you.

👁 Once you're situated, slowly unleash your senses:

Focus first on your sense of sight. Observe the Night's landscape, noticing what you see and what you don't. What stands out to you (and what doesn't)? What (or who) catches your attention? How do familiar things look in the darkness?

What does the Night sound like? Focus less on cars driving by or on your neighbor's dog barking and more on what exists in the sliver of moonlight in between all those noises. Try opening your eyes and closing them. Does this change what you hear? If the Night were a song, what song would it be? Do you hear creatures? Are they on the ground? In the sky? In a tree? Can you tell what they are just based on what you hear? Or is everything strange and unfamiliar in the blackness of Night?

How does the Night feel on your skin? Is it a blanket or a butterfly kiss? Is the Night air humid, playful, chilly?

Now use your nose. What do you smell standing under the Night sky? (Is it strange to be sniffing the Night? How does it feel for you, Firefly?)

Open your mouth and taste the Night. Yes, it will feel . . . unusual to try this. Do it anyway. Let the Night wrap around your tongue. Is it like anything you've eaten before?

Finally, open yourself fully to the Night, allowing all your senses to sing together. Gently notice how your Nighttime knowings differ from the knowings of your daytime self.

Who Are You in the Night?

Your Night-self is the mirror image of your daylight self. A lot of things about us are the same at Night, but often in the darkness, when no one is watching or judging us, we feel a little lighter and freer. Get to know the shimmer of your Night-self. Notice if you feel a little differently than you do by the light of day.

Now, in your heart, reach out to the Night. Ask what it has to share with you. The Night doesn't usually speak in words. When you ask it a question, the answer might flit across your mind or come to you through following where your attention leads. What's the first thought that dances across your brain when you ask the Night what it has to share with you? What catches your attention that you hadn't noticed before? Practice observing. Remember, you're not deciding whether these noticings are good or bad. Rather, you're just letting them land like snowflakes on your winter mittens.

💡 What do you think observing the Night and activating your senses has to do with magic?

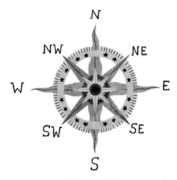

One Final Bit of Observation

There's one final thing we must do before we head inside, Firefly: We need to ground you in your Night Spot so you can always return home. You'll need your compass and your flashlight (unless you have a glow-in-the-dark compass).

Let's start by finding north. Hold your compass flat on your palm and click on your flashlight so you can see it. Notice how the needle floats within the compass casing. Move around a little bit so you can see the needle moving. Now look carefully: One end of the needle will be red.

We're getting to the tricky part, Firefly! Even though the needle moves around, the red end of the needle *always* points north! This can be confusing. For now, ignore the letters and words on your compass and only look at the needle. No matter what direction your body is facing, the red end of the needle will point north.

Now you're going to face north with your body. To do this, turn in a circle, continuing to hold your compass flat on your palm, until the little *N* on the compass is underneath the red end of the needle. Now *you* are facing north. Behind you is south. To your right is east and to your left is west. Phew! You did it!

Why is this important?

You're going to use these four compass points to ground you in your Night Spot so you can always find your way home. Since you're facing North, let's start there. Call on all your senses as you face North. Is the sky lighter or darker in this direction? Are there trees overhead or a streetlight in the distance? What do you hear and smell? Maybe there's a particular landmark like a mountain, an oak tree, a freeway, or a very tall building that you see? If you are at a window or on a porch, you may find that you're looking into your living room or kitchen. That's great: Whatever you see, hear, smell, taste, and feel is exactly right. Do this same exercise for each of the four directions.

Want to increase the magic of the moment? Look for the four elements— the building blocks of the mystical Universe—in the world around you. Is there a stream or a swimming pool nearby? That would be Water. Streetlights would be Fire. Wind chimes or anything else designed to sway in the breeze is Air. And you're probably sitting on a bit of Earth. Your Night Spot has a unique combination of elements. If you think hard, you'll probably realize all the elements are present.

When you are done with this exercise, you will be familiar with the uniqueness of your Night Spot and how it reads to all your senses. You will always be able to imagine it in your mind, which is what's important for our future field trips.

Record Your Findings in Two Different Ways

This is where your journal comes in, Firefly. As we take our Night School field trips, you'll want to record your thoughts and observations so you can go back to them later and give them extra attention and study.

When you're ready, head back indoors or close the window and turn on the lights. Tonight, we're going to record our observations by writing a Night Haiku and by creating a Night Collage.

Night Haiku

You may already know that a haiku is a type of short poem that originated in thirteenth-century Japan. Since haiku are only three lines long, they're the milk and cookies of the poetry world (just a quick snack, not a whole meal). Haiku are often about nature, so an ode to the Night or the four elements is common for these types of poems.

Start by thinking of a few words you can use to describe the sensations you smelled, tasted, and heard in your Night Spot. Use this as an excuse to string your words together in unexpected ways in order to create new meanings. Words that would never sit side by side during the day are perfectly comfortable hanging out together at Night: *sweet and grassy*; *cucumber and wood smoke*; *hoot and burp*.

Remember, a haiku is three lines long. The lines don't need to rhyme, but the number of syllables in each line does matter. You'll need to count the syllables as follows:

* ✳ five for the first line
* ✳ seven for the second line
* ✳ five for the third line

Knowing this, a Night Haiku might look something like this:

> *Hush, green frog burping!*
> *The hoot of a midnight owl*
> *warns: find grass and hide!*

Or:

> *The TV is on.*
> *Night, through the open window,*
> *Tastes of cucumbers.*

Your turn, Firefly.

In your journal, write a haiku or two describing the Night or your Night Spot, as well as notes on your observations from your trip outside. Easy peasy.

Too easy? If you want a challenge, try to include things to represent all four elements—Earth, Air, Water, and Fire—in your haiku!

Night Collage

Images speak to us in a way that's different than words. They crack open the door to the land of symbols, which we will be working with later in the Night School.

Let's begin by finding images that have a Nighttime *mood*, Firefly. What I mean by this is, instead of looking for Nighttime pictures, seek out images that make you *feel* the way you did outside in the dark. For example, if you felt peaceful in your Night Spot, you might choose a picture of a sleeping puppy. Or maybe the color blue feels like peace, and you'll select a photo of a lake or ocean. Choose images that remind you of your feelings. You can cut these images from magazines or print them from a computer. If you like to work online, you can search for an app to make what's called a "mood board" (which is what people call a collection of images meant to create a certain feeling).

Your collage will take more than a single evening to complete. Tonight, make a start by looking at images. Over the weeks to come you can select the ones that speak to you and begin to arrange your creation.

How and where you arrange your collage is completely up to your own creative instincts. (Yes, you have creative instincts! If they have been dormant, they should consider this their invitation to poke their heads up and sniff the stars.) You could tape images to a window in your living room or to the mirror in your bathroom. You could use a tabletop as your canvas and arrange images and objects upon it. You could use paint or markers or colored pencils to add words to the collage in your notebook. Try adding some glitter for a magical sparkle, or glue down dried leaves. Perhaps your collage will be swaths of color, which relate to what you tasted in the Night air or doodles you create to mimic the way the clouds moved against the moon.

This collage might take months to fully complete—an ever-growing work of wonder that you can return to in the daytime to help you remember the feeling of the Night and who you became when you stepped into it for the first time.

MS. MARLOWE'S MAGICAL LIBRARY: STUDY THE PHILOSOPHY OF MAGIC

YOU ARE

CORDIALLY INVITED

TO TOUR THE LIBRARY OF

Ms. Beatrice Marlowe

**HOT CHOCOLATE AND COOKIES
TO BE SERVED AFTERWARD**

WHEN: Ten minutes after the first star appears
WHERE: Ms. Marlowe's Magical Library

*Note: Please inform
your parents of your visit!*

🎒 You'll need your notebook . . . and that's it!

SPECIAL INSTRUCTIONS:

When the first star appears, go to the place
you've chosen where you can feel the Night sky—
your Night Spot. Use your compass to face east.
Settle yourself in a seated position and close
your eyes. In your mind, imagine a house. The
house is sitting high on a cliff. You can hear
the ocean waves crashing below. The house is
rather unusual: It's more a collection of small
buildings connected each to each by courtyards
and walkways than a single home. The buildings
themselves are a strange and whimsical hodgepodge
of architecture: old stone farm buildings snuggle
up to modern glass breezeways. Blooming roses
and honeysuckle adorn the walls. Owls hoot in
the distance. A well-lit path winds through the
compound. In your mind, you follow the path to
the second building on the right. The door will
be propped open. Enter and come down the circular
stairway to the high-domed library, where you
will see Ms. Marlowe waiting. . . .

Welcome, Firefly!

I am so excited to introduce you to my library!

The books on these shelves were handed down to me by the last Night School head teacher, who inherited them from the head teacher before him. Someday I'll pass them along to whomever leads the school after me. These books are not only a part of the Night School's past, but also a link to our future. And isn't that just mind-boggling to contemplate? Think of the many teachers and students who have touched these books and those who will touch them in years to come. *You* are now a part of that story.

You can't help but notice, as you come down the staircase, that this library is located underground. Sunlight, while wonderful for reading, is not ideal for old books. Dampness is also terrible for manuscripts, and we all know basements are prone to dampness. The hum you're hearing is the system that controls humidity. Dry and dark, that's how books like it!

Now come this way. Let's gather around the library table. You can see there are some books here that are in the process of being repaired.

💡 Why, you might wonder, do we need so many books? And why work so hard to preserve them?

Books are a place to store ideas, Firefly. They are how we remember the thoughts of people long past. And people have a lot of thoughts. Some of them are useful, some of them are silly, and some of them are terribly destructive. A few thoughts and ideas will become common, and many people think them. But the *common* thoughts are not always the *correct* thoughts. For example, for centuries people were certain that the sun rotated around the Earth. That thought was so universally shared that you'd be considered crazy if you thought differently.

But it turns out that thought was wrong. We now know that the Earth revolves around the sun.

So it's important to keep track of thoughts and ideas because a thought that seems wrong today may be the exact thought we need tomorrow!

And a library is a place to store and organize all these thoughts. It's where you can go to learn how other people think.

BRAINSTORM A LIST OF INCORRECT THOUGHTS

Consider what other thoughts and ideas might have seemed right at one point in history but were later found to be incorrect. Maybe they were ideas based upon incorrect facts or maybe the ideas were found to be unkind or unfair ways of thinking. See if you can come up with three examples and feel free to write them in your notebook for safekeeping.

Ready to explore a few thousand years of other people's thinking? Let's take a stroll through the stacks—*stacks* is librarian-speak for *bookshelves*!

Come right this way and be with the books for a moment. Most libraries are arranged by topic, but I've set mine up chronologically. Do you know the word *chronologically? Chronos* tells us that the word has something to do with time and how time passes. And I'm sure you know the word *logically.* So, setting up the library *chrono-logically* means arranging it by the logic of time. We are in the center of the library. The shelves spiral out from here. Nearest to us are the oldest books, while the newest are farthest out. Don't worry, there are cut-throughs between these centuries. You needn't walk the whole spiral to get from books written in Ancient Egypt to those penned in modern-day Mexico.

One of my favorite library activities, Firefly, is pulling a random book off the shelf and seeing what it has to share. Some books are terribly chatty; others not so much. Conversing with books is the best part of a library experience.

Did you see what I just did there?

I implied that books are *alive*. And I believe they are, in their own bookish way.

This idea—that everything is alive, even objects like books and rocks—is called *animism*. Animism is the belief that there's a spiritual essence in all things. Another way of saying that would be: *Everything holds the creative energy of its own beginning.*

It's easy to understand this concept when we look at a baby bird or even a work of art. It's harder to find that spark in mass-produced objects like toaster ovens and cell phones. But it's there!

EXPLORE ANIMISM

Can you think of an inanimate object that has felt alive to you? Maybe a stuffed animal, which you named and talked to as a younger child? Or perhaps an old tablet, which you need to encourage a little so search results come up quickly? Looking for the spark makes it easy to find magic in all the parts of your Night-life; when seen this way, the world comes alive!

This sense of being alive is what I feel when I walk between the shelves of a library. Let's chat up a few books, shall we? I'll just pull one down now, open it to a random page, and read you a sentence:

ποταμοῖσι τοῖσιν αὐτοῖσιν ἐμβαίνουσιν ἕτερα καὶ ἕτερα ὕδατα ἐπιρρεῖ

Oh dear! That's ancient Greek, Firefly. I forgot this whole section is written in older languages! Let's see if I can translate this phrase. Hmmmm . . . It roughly means:

No one ever steps into the same river twice.

This is the rather famous thought of a man named Heraclitus, a Greek philosopher from a very long time ago, so long ago they aren't sure of his exact birthday (it's thought to be around 544 BCE).

What do you think he means when he says that you can't step into the same river twice? I'm sure you've swum in a swimming pool or the ocean and then gone back the next year and swum in the same swimming pool or ocean. It's the same, right?

Or is it?

Let's look at this idea a little more closely. Say you're about to step into a powerful river, like the Nile. Let's also say that you have visited this particular riverbank before. Now go one step further and speculate that the stars are in the exact same place on the horizon and the same palm trees are sighing in a gentle breeze, just like they were the last time you dipped a toe into this mighty river. In your mind, you're stepping into the same river.

But are you, Firefly?

The water molecules that swirled around your ankles when you last visited have long since sped out to sea. The exact particles of silt that squished between your toes are probably now part of the seabed of the Mediterranean, possibly miles from where you currently stand. Even though your goal was to return to this exact spot on the Nile, as you can see it's no longer the *exact* same spot.

Now how about you? Are you the exact same *you*, Firefly?

Not a chance! For one, your body is constantly changing all the way down to your cells. You make new white blood cells every couple of days, and the cells in your liver change over once a year. Just like the river, some parts of you are the same . . . but some parts are very different.

Just like you can't completely be the same person you were a year ago, you can't step in the same river—or garden, or beach, or train station— twice because *change* is always happening.

And this, Firefly, brings us to one of the fundamental principles of magic:

Go with the flow!

When we use animism to see the world around us as alive and then we apply Heraclitus's theory that everything is changing, we begin to realize that the world around us is a very active place. Our brains often forget this. We look at the sky, Night after Night, and think, *It looks the same as yesterday evening.* But when we pay closer attention, we realize this isn't true: The Night sky is always moving and changing. The trick is to pay attention so we can notice which direction the change is going.

Luckily, this is not a guessing game. Close observation will show you which way things are headed. For example, if you look up at the Night sky for a few evenings in a row, you can see whether the moon is waxing— which means getting bigger—or waning—which means getting smaller.

Now, here's where the magic comes in: You, too, are part of this pattern of change. And if you *go with the flow*, you're beginning to work with the patterns around you. You become a part of the dance. And that's pure magic.

Let's say you're wanting to make something bigger, like your circle of friends. The best time to begin working on this project would be at the new moon because from new moon to full moon, the energy in the Night sky is expanding. And this matches the energy you want to bring to your social circle: You want it to grow!

How about if you want to make something smaller? Like the clutter in your bedroom or the amount of homework you get from your math teacher?

If you want to make things shrink, it's best to work on this at the time when the energy in the world around you is also getting smaller. That would be when the moon is waning.

👁 What else waxes and wanes, Firefly? Start noticing!

I'm sure you're itching to see where the moon is right now, which is difficult since we're in an underground library! I have just a little bit of homework for you before I return you to your Night Spot so you can check out where the moon is in its cycle.

TAKE NOTES FROM YOUR LIBRARY VISIT

We've covered quite a bit this evening! The Law of Forgetfulness tells us that we must write things down to help ourselves remember them. In your journal, please make notes on:

- Your thoughts on animism and change.
- The patterns of the moon (and anything else you might think of that also waxes and wanes!).

That, I believe is more than enough for one evening. Let's gather for hot chocolate and cookies, and I'll tell you how to return home to your Night Spot.

You got to my library, Firefly, by a process called visualization. You're going to go home the same way. I realize it would be very easy to skip this part—to just put down this book and go about your evening. But, instead, I'd like you to reverse the process that got you here. Visualize your way home. I'm having you do this as practice, Firefly, so you create solid habits for when you do higher magics. While advanced magics are beyond the scope of our studies here, good habits will make it easier for you later!

So, when you're ready, close your eyes and picture the library with its spiral staircase through the center. Begin climbing up the way you came down. In the foyer, you'll find the door open to the courtyard outside. The path is lit with small twinkly lights, and you can easily follow it back toward the place you started—your Night Spot. When you get to the place in your visualization where you are back in your own space, open your eyes, stand up, and give your body a stretch.

Well done, Firefly! We're going a bit farther away on our next field trip—all the way to a country called Greece, where the Night School has a secondary campus. I can't wait to see you there!

THE MYSTERY SCHOOL OF YOU:
MEET THE MYSTIC WITHIN

Ready, Firefly? We're about to take a big trip! You'll be spending a week at the Night School's campus in Greece to participate in a *Mystery School.*

Sounds mysterious, doesn't it?

And it's supposed to! Mystery Schools are ancient classrooms for teaching what today we might call **spirituality**, philosophy, and magic. The first Mystery School was held before 3000 BCE, and these schools are known to have existed in Egypt, India, and Iraq. *You* are now about to become a part of this long history.

So, gather your journal and get ready to depart!

🎒 **You'll need your notebook . . . and a bit of imagination!**

Head to your Night Spot and allow the darkness to soften your sight. I'll meet you at the Temple of Apollo in Delphi, Greece. Don't worry if you've never been there. The lovely thing about traveling by visualization is that all you need is a picture of the place you want to go to! And, since visualization is not affected by the usual rules of time, let's travel back to when the Temple of Apollo was still standing. (It's in ruins now, which makes it hard to find a clean place to sit down!)

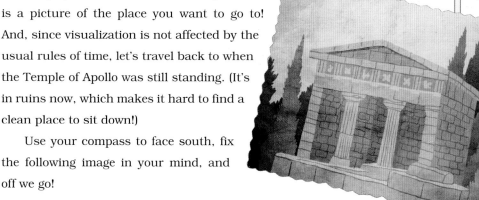

Use your compass to face south, fix the following image in your mind, and off we go!

Welcome, Firefly!

Well done getting yourself here. That was some excellent visualizing!

It's time to begin a journey into the mysterious world of *you*. We'll be starting here, at the Temple of Apollo in Delphi where we will then be meeting for lessons for the next five Nights. Each Night, head to your Night Spot and visualize your way here, like you just did tonight. Don't worry—there's an **amphitheater** around back where we can sit for our lessons!

Let me quickly go over your Night School Mystery School syllabus:

✱ **NIGHT 1**: Know Thyself

✱ **NIGHT 2**: Me and We

✱ **NIGHT 3**: Nurture vs. Magical Nature

✱ **NIGHT 4**: Your Personal Path into the Magic

✱ **NIGHT 5**: The Power of Purpose

NIGHT 1: KNOW THYSELF

Imagine, if you will, the light of the full moon shining on the chiseled columns as we climb the marble steps to the **portico** of the Temple of Apollo, where we are confronted with this message:

In case your Ancient Greek is rusty, that loosely translates to:

KNOW THYSELF

NOTHING IN EXCESS

SURETY BRINGS RUIN

Eh?

Scholars have been debating that last *E* for centuries. Did the stone-mason leave for lunch, mid-carving, and never return? Was he thinking about his sweetheart, Electra, and in his distraction began carving her name?

My personal take is that it's not a letter but, instead, a glyph—an illustration—of how we should interact with the other three sentences. This glyph, which looks like an *E*, represents the three lines of thought above connected by an upright line, which I understand as a reminder to connect the previous three phrases within ourselves.

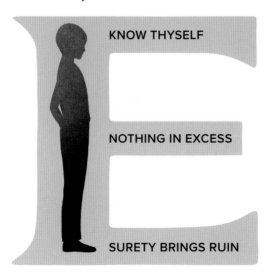

KNOW THYSELF

NOTHING IN EXCESS

SURETY BRINGS RUIN

This idea of being upright—meaning upstanding and moral—was foundational to becoming a student at any of the ancient Mystery Schools. The Mysteries were open only to those who had first mastered themselves.

Mastering yourself means being thoughtful about your feelings and impulses. A person who has mastered their feelings doesn't just start yelling when they get angry. Instead they pause and think about their emotions and what they want to say to the people around them. Someone who has mastered their own impulses understands that what we want isn't always what's best for us: For example, sometimes you want another cookie even though you know one more super-duper-fudgy-chunk-chip will give you a bellyache. A person who has mastered themselves will not eat that extra cookie! They realize that even though they want it, it won't be good for them.

💡 Think about why the ancient Mystery Schools insisted that students have self-mastery. What do you think self-mastery has to do with mysticism?

So here we are, Firefly, standing on the threshold of the Temple of Apollo at Delphi, where in ancient times the most famous oracle in the world worked. An oracle is a bit like a fortune teller, and the Oracle of Delphi was the best of the best. All types of people—from kings to farmers—would come here when life felt confusing or uncertain.

But look up again on the temple wall! The inscription reads: KNOW THYSELF, NOTHING IN EXCESS, SURETY BRINGS RUIN. When you arrive at the temple where the oracle works, instead of being reassured that you'll be given an answer, you are instead reminded to first know yourself . . . and then to question even that. Self-knowledge was considered so absolutely necessary in ancient times that people were reminded of it before going inside the temple to have their fortune told.

Why was knowing yourself so important? you might wonder.

Because prophecies, like much you will encounter when you put on your Night-goggles, are delivered in the language of stories and symbols. The meaning is all in the interpretation, and *you* are going to be the person doing that interpretation! You need to understand your thought patterns and be able to stop yourself from jumping to conclusions when you are thinking about mystical things.

Back at the temple, if you were wanting to seek out the words of the oracle, you would pay the admission price and line up with the other travelers to ask your question. After months of anticipation as you journeyed by boat or horse or on foot to get here, imagine how you'd feel when the Pythia (that's the name of the high priestess at the Temple, Firefly) said something like: *The golden strawberry is in the mouth of spring's first snake.*

What? That prophecy is gobbledygook! You traveled weeks and paid good gold and then all you got were snakes and strawberries!

And then, in the middle of your internal rant, you remember that you were told to *Know Thyself.*

So you pause and think. What does a strawberry mean to you? How about a snake?

Knowing yourself is suddenly very important. You realize that *you* are the filter through which this prophecy will be interpreted.

Here's another way to think of it, Firefly: Imagine you're stargazing and your telescope has a small smudge just to the right of the center point. Because of that smudge, every star you gaze upon has a small smudge just to the right of it. You might spend years developing a theory of why stars create dust clouds on their right side.

Wouldn't you feel foolish, after years of thinking about this, to realize that the stars aren't actually smudged, but your telescope is?

Standing befuddled outside the Temple of Apollo, you realize that you are just like that telescope. You need to know where your smudges are. You need to understand your focal length and your magnification. Everything you study or learn is filtered through the telescope of your perception, which is made up of your thoughts, feelings, beliefs, smells, sounds, tastes, prejudices, blind spots, and *stories*. Oh, so many stories that you tell yourself about who you are, how you feel about your family, whether you connect with other kids at school, what you know about the doings in the larger world . . . You're made up of stories, stacked one atop the other, creating a mental and emotional city only you can map.

That is the purpose of this Mystery School: to begin to map the stories that make up your own magical identity. Because how you live within these stories influences your perception of the world around you. And how the world around you (with its own collection of stories) views you also has a way of changing the way you see things.

Picking apart these layers is the only way to make sense of the snakes, strawberries, and other symbols that are the lifeblood of the mystic. The folks who built the Temple of Apollo at Delphi knew this, and now, hopefully, so do you!

💡 For the next week of Mystery School, let's work with a process that can help you know a little more about how your heart ticks and your brain tocks. Whenever a strong thought, sensation, or emotion crosses your mind, ask yourself: *Really? Why?* Don't overthink this. Trust that the first thing your internal voice says is true even if you don't understand it.

So maybe you think, *I hate ice cream.*

Then ask yourself, *Really? Why?*

If you answer, *Yes, really, it hurts my stomach*, or *Yes, really, the feeling of eating it is revolting*, then (surprise, surprise) you really *do* hate ice cream.

But what if you ask yourself *Really? Why?* and you realize that you can't remember what ice cream tastes like? What you recall instead is that you stopped eating ice cream a long time ago when you were a little kid, because your brother, who is lactose intolerant, would look at you with sad puppy eyes every time you ate it in front of him. So you just stopped eating it, because you hated to see your brother looking so sad. When people asked if you wanted ice cream, you would simply mumble something about not liking it. You said it so many times that it started to feel true. But when you get to the root of it, you realize that maybe it's not.

What do you think you know about yourself that might actually not be true? This is your week to find out!

That's it for tonight, Firefly. For the next four Nights, we'll meet in the amphitheater in the back of the Temple. I trust that you can do the visualization to get here by yourself, then just walk around back and you'll see me. We'll jump right into class each Night. While lessons will be shorter than this one, there will be activities with each, so prepare yourself!

NIGHT 2: ME AND WE

Welcome back, Firefly!

I have a fascinating study to share to start our discussion this evening:

Two gentlemen—by the names of Nicholas Christakis and James Fowler—looked at thirty years of data on social networks. What they learned, Firefly, is that you are influenced not only by the people closest to you but also by the people who influence those people. This means you are affected by those around you . . . even the people you don't know!

Who is influencing your thoughts and attitudes, Firefly? And, more importantly, is their influence supporting your highest self and helping you become the person you want to be? Are you surrounded by people who understand the power of symbols and signs, or by people who make you doubt yourself and question the magic of the world?

It's time to find out!

Inventory Your Influencers

From television to the friend you eat lunch with to ideas on the internet, you are surrounded by other people's thoughts and feelings. Who is influencing you, and what is the nature of their influence? For this homework assignment, you'll be making a list. This is not just a list of family and friends; this is also a list of characters on the TV shows you watch and those in the books you choose to read. If you are on social media, it's the people you encounter there as well.

After looking at this list, highlight the influencers that support your well-being, happiness, and your sense of magic in the world. In other words, which of these people and/or characters leave a positive stamp on your life?

EXTRA CREDIT: Now that you have a list of who is affecting your mood and magical mindset, buff and polish your influencer list for greater success! If you have friends who are unkind or unsupportive or if you are listening to people who make you feel small, think about how you can spend more time with people who make you feel good about yourself and encourage your dreams.

Remember, this is not about only hanging out with people who agree with you! Take a lesson from the ancient philosophers and, each week, have at least one debate with someone who maybe sees things differently than you. Seek out people who challenge you in ways that make you think and feel more deeply. Let them light a fire within you for exploring fresh ideas and diving further into the mysteries of life.

NIGHT 3: NURTURE VS. MAGICAL NATURE

The modern world is sometimes unfriendly to the imaginative, magical part of our being, Firefly. Because of this, you may have decided it was safer or smarter to hide your mystical side. Early experiences might have shaped the way you see the world and how you have felt about exploring life's mysteries. Sifting through the events in your life that have made you want to hide will help you to begin to unknot your own magic.

Tonight, you are the storyteller. Your job this evening is to begin to remember what the magic in your nature looked and felt like when you were younger.

This is a tale only you can tell, so pull out your journal and let's get right to work!

Your Story

Think about the ways in which your early ideas about the mystic were changed or somehow made "normal." Or, if you are one of the lucky ones who were encouraged to grow into the world of magic and mystery, reflect on how your ideas or thoughts have grown over time.

Think about:

1. What you thought about magic when you were young
2. How imagination has factored into your life
3. Experiences of "seeing" things: ghosts, invisible friends, fairies
4. Trance-like experiences
5. Dreams you remember
6. The desire to explore things like astrology or tarot

Now think about how the people in your life responded when you shared these experiences:

1. Were you told you were "so cute" or "so creative"?
2. Did you hear "you have a magnificent imagination," not as encouragement, but as a line drawn to keep imagination from interfering with the "real world"?
3. Were you shushed and told you didn't hear what you thought you heard or didn't see what you thought you saw?
4. Were you told your attraction to the mystical tools and channels was evil or against the will of God?
5. Were you expected not to waste your time exploring things like astrology or tarot?

(It's okay to be thinking *No, Ms. Marlowe, it wasn't like that for me at all!* If that's what you're thinking, use this writing time to share what it was like for you!)

If you had any of these experiences, how did they alter how you inter-acted with or felt magic for yourself? What walls did you put up as a result?

Investigate thoughts that feel defensive or that hurt you. This can be painful, Firefly. Still, it's an important part of knowing yourself. Sometimes it helps to imagine you are your older self comforting your younger self. Using your imagination in this way lets you explore hurtful topics while also accessing your own inner fortitude (*fortitude*, Firefly, is a fancy word for strength).

In summation, tonight's homework is a step toward peeling back the blankets that might be covering the magic within you. When you are through this exercise, a good cry for your past self might be in order. Tears are magic: water for flow and salt for protection, pulling out pain and puri-fying you for what comes next.

NIGHT 4: YOUR PERSONAL PATH INTO THE MAGIC

Magic shows up daily in each of our lives. Let's learn some language to help us better recognize that magic every day!

A large part of who you are as a seeker of the mysteries of the Night will be determined by how you personally perceive the magic of the world around you. Do you see colors around people (those are called **auras**)? Do you speak with ghosts? These first two examples are very obviously magical. But there are more subtle magics, Firefly! Maybe you always know the best moment to ask your mom a tough question or sense who is on the phone before it rings. Perhaps you navigate the internet with ease, always intuitively knowing which terms to use in a web search.

Each of these skills, and dozens of others, comes from having an awareness of the world around you that reaches beyond the five senses (taste, smell, touch, sight, and hearing). Did you know that everyone has a sixth sense? They do! That sixth sense is an ability to take in information by reading the energy patterns around a particular person, place, or experience. (Remember, Firefly, energy is the stuff you can sense but can't physically see or hear.)

But while everyone has a sixth sense, the ways in which you interpret the energetic information you receive is unique to you. Because patterns of energy have no language, your brain translates them into something you find more understandable. For some people that means experiencing visions; for others it's hearing voices or understanding patterns or feeling information in their own body.

There are some words that can help you explore the range of possibilities for interpreting energetic information. I fondly refer to these words as *the Clairs*.

THE CLAIRS

Clairvoyance: Clairvoyance is associated with your third eye, the eye that sees not the physical world, but the spiritual one. If you see auras or can describe the style of your childhood "imaginary" friend's clothing, then clairvoyance is a tool you use to make sense of the information you're getting from the unseen world.

Clairaudience: Did you imagine your stuffed animals talking to you when you were younger? Or, when you're thinking of a problem, does a song that seems to answer your questions just happen to play in your head? If so, you are interpreting the energies of the world with clairaudience, which means your brain is translating the invisible patterns of the world into sound.

Claircognizance: Do you recognize patterns easily? Or perhaps you discover you know the answer to a problem without knowing how you know it? You might know who is calling before the phone rings or sense a parent has come home before their key turns in the lock. This is claircognizance: clear knowing.

Clairsentience: Those who are clairsentient feel things in their bodies. If your palms always itch when your teacher is angry, or you sneeze when someone lies to you, then you are displaying clairsentience. This can be a difficult Clair to recognize! If you suspect you are clairsentient, keeping a journal noting physical sensations and what is happening in the world around you when these sensations are happening can help you figure out how your physical sensations are conveying information.

Clairalience and **Clairgustance**: These fabulous Clairs are a little less common. Clairalience is when your brain translates the energy patterns you perceive as scent, while clairgustance reveals energies as taste. If you are meditating and suddenly smell your grandpa's aftershave, or if you always taste saltwater taffy before a thunderstorm, you're likely familiar with these less usual Clairs!

By the light of day, the Clairs might feel like fairy godmothers: the wispy dream of a mystical imagination. But by the shine of the stars, when objects and ideas soften around the edges, they will come and kiss you on the cheek, reminding you of a depth of knowing you may have forgotten you have.

Still, it's easy for the mind to feel doubtful. If yours does, feed it this factoid: Synesthesia, a condition recognized by modern medicine and science, means one of the five senses automatically triggers a second. So, for a synesthete, sound might be translated into color, taste, or scent. And next to this bit of magic, the Clairs seem positively ordinary!

Consider Your Magics

Let's uncover more about your mystical potential!

This evening, you're going to make a list of your earliest memories of things that felt magical. Did you see fairies? Hear voices? Have an invisible friend or talk to the family cat? Did you know who was coming to visit before they showed up at your door unexpectedly? Have your journal handy so you can record your memories.

Ready to get started?

If so, close your eyes and breathe steadily, in and out. Count backward from your current age to the age of five. Each breath represents one year as you wind back time and revisit your past self. When you get to five, sit with your five-year-old self and remember. How did you see the world? How did you let the magic in?

After you have recorded what you have learned, count yourself back up to your present age.

This last bit is important, Firefly. Get into the habit of returning to your starting point so that your spirit fully returns to your body whenever you put yourself in a light trance like this. You want to always bring yourself back to the present time and place, which is why I have told you to visualize yourself back to your Night Spot after you complete each lesson!

NIGHT 5: THE POWER OF PURPOSE

As we wrap up our Mystery School studies, Firefly, I want to pose some final questions:

💡 What will you do with the magic you discover at the Night School? Why is the mystic appealing to you?

Be honest with yourself about what you are seeking when you reach into the Night. Your desires are part of who you are and will help guide you in your future magical quests.

There are so many ways to bring your Night studies into the daylight world. This is your invitation to begin noodling on this topic. Offer a gentle invitation for your own answers to come out and play over the coming weeks!

You don't have to know all the answers to everything today. Sit with these questions—*be* with the questions. Imagine they are seeds you have planted to help yourself grow.

And it's a wrap, Firefly! As a graduate of Mystery School, you are now ready to drink the Moon Juice and learn some real magic. I can't wait to see you for our next field trip, where you will learn how to set an intention, cast a spell, and create a **ritual**!

Don't forget to visualize your way back to your Night Spot. Good habits make good magic!

field trip NO.4

THE WORLD HEADQUARTERS OF WITCHERY MARKETING, LLC: CAST A SPELL!

Ready for another field trip, Firefly? Tonight, we're going to New York City to visit a very dear friend of mine, Morgan Fay. Morgan—that's Ms. Fay to you—and I were Night School students together. Now she runs a fabulously famous marketing firm in Manhattan. As a CEO (that's chief executive officer, Firefly), she has a unique take on magic. She uses it quite successfully in her business ventures, and she's very excited to share her secrets with you this evening!

If you know your way around Manhattan, use your compass to face north, then visualize your way to the Washington Square arch. If you're new to the city, here's a picture to guide you on your way! Add the scents of fried food and car exhaust, and you'll be all set. Morgan's office is hidden behind a few charms, so I'll walk you in after we get there!

🎒 **You'll need your notebook . . . and an open mind!**

Hello, Firefly! You made it!

Ah, New York City at Night. Let's open our senses so we can take it in!

Notice that you can't see the stars here, Firefly. Instead, we are surrounded by our own brilliance—electric light. I think what we're smelling is a spicy curry from the restaurant around the corner. And, of course, we're hearing the particular Night noises of Manhattan: car engines and horns, people's voices, and—because we're in Washington Square Park—a bit of music. It seems there's always someone hanging out with a guitar here. All of these sensations help us to remember that the Night is not just one thing. It might be a quiet hush where you live, Firefly, but here it's a carnival!

Come this way. No, I'm not giving you street names—Morgan doesn't like unexpected visitors! Let's walk through this gate. The walls are narrow back here—I always scrape my shoulders on the stones! But here we are: Morgan's garden. It always amazes me what she can grow right here in the city. Morgan is what we call a "Green Witch." That means she works with plants and elements from nature. If you want to impress her, Firefly, show off your knowledge of the four elements!

Ah! Here she comes now! I'm going to relax on this lovely bench and let Ms. Fay take it from here!

Welcome, Night School students! I'm thrilled you could join me this evening. My name is Morgan Fay, and despite what Ms. Marlowe says, you can just call me Morgan. I am the CEO of Witchery. We're a marketing firm that works with a handful of very select clients. You might have heard of some of them—Hedgewitch Goods & Garden? The Conservancy for the Protection of Wild Dragons? No? Well, suffice to say, I must be careful who I work with because when you work with Witchery there's always a little magic in the mix. So, I only take clients whose purpose I deeply believe in because you should only use magic in alignment with your values. And when you start working with magic out in the world, you must think about not just *your* purpose but the purpose of all the folks you work with!

Tonight, you are here to learn about spells. These are one of my favorite magics! Why, you might be wondering, did Ms. Marlowe bring you here? She could have easily taught you about spells herself. Trust me when I say she's quite skilled in this area! But she tells me that, being a businesswoman, I have a unique perspective to offer, so here you are!

Let's start with a little bit about me. After attending the Night School, I went on to get my MBA (which stands for master of business administration). MBA programs are not mysterious at all (most of the students are pure Daylighters!). So, imagine my surprise when we had a lecture on setting goals that sounded remarkably similar to how I'd learned to set intentions at the Night School! Setting an intention is the first step in casting a spell, and, it turns out, Daylighters do it all the time. It made me aware that the kind of magic we do might be more commonplace than I had realized, and that different people were simply calling the same actions by a variety of names. Sometimes you might have to change your language when you're working in the daylight world . . . but that doesn't mean you have to forget your magic!

Okay, class! Let's learn how to cast a spell!

As I mentioned, a spell begins as a thought exercise called *setting an intention.*

What, you might wonder, is an intention?

An intention is like a wish, but with a bit more oomph behind it! It's a specific thing you'd like to have happen. In business school we called them *goals* or *outcomes.*

Now we get to the tricky part:

Your **energy** follows your **intentions**.

Let's break that statement down, shall we? You have energy. You use it to do all sorts of things: thinking, walking the dog, talking with your friends. Where your energy goes is determined by your intentions. This is easily understood in the physical world: When I go out in the garden with the intention to pull the weeds, my physical energy goes into actually pulling weeds! This same idea—that your energy follows your intention—applies to spiritual and psychic energy, which is the kind of energy we use for casting spells. While this type of energy is hard to see, it's pretty easy to sense once you start searching for it.

👁 Let's pause for a moment and observe our own energy. Because it's hard to see, we need to *feel* it! To do that, let's begin by briskly rubbing our hands together. Do this for a count of twenty. First, you'll notice your palms getting warm. Heat is a kind of energy. Now, take your warm hands and hold them over your open eyes, not quite touching.

(Why your eyes and not your nose or mouth? The skin around your eyes is sensitive, which makes this exercise easier.)

Observe what you notice in the space between your hands and your eyes. At first it might just be warmth. See if you feel or notice anything else!

As you move forward with our magical lessons, keep these sensations in mind to help you remember that there are things in the world that are difficult to see or hear or smell, but you can still *sense* them! At the Night School, we call the invisible things that cause these sensations *energy*.

Take a deep breath and come back to attention, please. Ah! That's it, your attention is on me, and I can feel your energy on me as well. Excellent!

Let's explore intentions and how they control our *attention*. Bear with me, Night Schoolers. I know you want to get to the magic, but I promise this all plays a part in getting you to the point where you can cast a spell!

So, intention and attention. On the most basic level, you will see *more* of whatever your mind is focusing upon. For instance, let's say you pull a tarot or oracle card (more on both in a later field trip—for a sneak peek, flip ahead to page 96) that features a bird. As you go about your evening, you might continue to think about the bird on the card and wonder what it means. Perhaps you start searching on the internet trying to figure out what kind of bird it is. Because your brain is focused on birds (in other words, birds have your *attention*), chances are you'll start noticing birds all around you! You'll see them as you walk to a friend's house, realize there's a bird's wing worked into the design of your favorite pillowcase (how had you missed that before?), and maybe even come across a feather, left seemingly right in your path, when you're out for a full-moon stroll. Now that I have you thinking about birds, you might even notice a wee saw-whet owl in the hawthorn in the corner of my garden.

These kinds of encounters—when the exact thing you're focusing on begins to appear in your life—always feel magical, especially when you're thinking positive thoughts. But the same principle applies when your thoughts are negative. For example, if you're thinking about people being mean to you, you're far more likely to interpret someone's silly comment as cruel instead of just foolish or thoughtless. So, what you *allow* yourself to think is incredibly important!

The first step to casting a solid spell is controlling your attention. But how do you stop your brain from going to places you'd rather it didn't? How can you control what you think?

> 👁 Begin by observing! Close your eyes. Pretend you're a detective and your job is to notice all the different types of thoughts that are in your brain right now.

I suspect, if you're anything like me, that when you drop into your mind unannounced, you find there are a lot of thoughts flying around. It can get very messy in a normal human brain! But there are skills you can learn to help quiet and organize your mind. Here are a few I'd like you to consider:

1. Meditation

Meditation is an age-old tradition that helps you achieve inner stillness. A simple way to begin meditating is to find a comfortable place to sit or lie down, close your eyes, and focus your attention on your own breath. Can you feel the air brushing across the little divot under your nose? Follow your breath in and out, noticing the sensations. You can say the word *inhale* as you breathe in and *exhale* as you breathe out. Repeating words like this is known as a *mantra*. Mantras are used to help you focus. While this all sounds easy, try meditating for just one minute and you'll realize it's harder than it seems!

2. Gratitude

Did you know you can train your brain? You can teach yourself to favor one type of thought over another. One of the best ways to do this is to keep a gratitude journal. This practice is very common in the daylight world, so if someone sees your gratitude journal in your school bag, it's no big deal! Plus, this is an easy practice: As you go about your day, notice things that make you smile. They could be very small things like the way the sunlight looks on tree leaves or the clumsiness of a puppy tumbling about. Every Night before bed, note these things in your journal. Your journal entry does not have to be long or fancy. A simple *I'm grateful there was pizza for lunch!* or *I'm grateful my friend gave me a hug* is all it takes. In this way, you teach your mind to pay more attention to the wonderful things in your life than the not-so-nice things. If you need a reminder, you can pull out your journal and read the things that have brought you joy.

3. Jogging (or jumping rope or dancing or riding a horse)

Rhythm can help hush your brain. Choose a repeating motion to focus on (this is similar to using a mantra in meditation). For example, when you are jogging you can focus on the in and out of your breath or the pumping of your legs.

4. Stepping outside yourself

Sometimes you need a little distance from your own thoughts and feelings to see them clearly. This exercise will help. Stepping outside yourself has degrees. You can take a little half step outside of yourself, which is what we're going to learn to do here, or you can take a full step outside of yourself, which puts you in the realm of astral travel. This is advanced magic and a bit much to accomplish without a spotter!

Let's work at taking a half step away from your busy brain. Begin by sitting quietly and focusing on your breath, just like in meditation. Allow your thoughts to flow through your mind. Notice them passing by but try not to focus on them. Your thoughts will want your attention (and therefore your energy!). Regard them as if they are restless children, let them know you hear them and will think about whatever they have to say later.

Oh, you're right! you might think. *A very important point. Let's give that some thought later tonight. Right now, we are practicing sitting quietly.*

This bit of active imagining may not feel exactly like meditating, but it will quickly get you to your actual goal: stepping outside and observing yourself.

As you practice acknowledging your racing thoughts, you'll start to gain the ability to observe your thinking mind without getting entangled in your own ponderings. Your spirit will notice that your mind is doing its never-ending-thinking thing but will also recognize that all that thinking doesn't have to ruffle your calm. You can observe yourself, and through observing begin to see that your mind is a part of you, but it's not *all* of you.

Having a quiet and orderly brain allows you to be thoughtful when you're setting your intentions, which is the first part of creating a spell.

As a cautionary tale, let's look at what happens when you are *not* calm and methodical and instead voice a desire, willy-nilly!

Here's an example:

> In a somewhat silly tale from Sweden, a woman is granted
> three wishes. Knowing her husband will come home hungry,
> she wishes for a sausage. Her husband arrives, and she tells
> him of the wishes and presents the sausage. The man gets very
> angry. "You had three wishes and you wasted one on a sausage?
> I wish that sausage was stuck to your nose!" he hollers. And
> the sausage sticks to her nose. The couple must then waste
> the last wish removing the sausage.

Fairy tales are a fabulous place to find out what happens when wishing goes wrong. Often, the person making the wish gets *exactly* what they ask for . . . only to find it's not what they want at all! It's obvious that if the husband had bothered to quiet his thoughts, the second and third wishes could have been better chosen. But this is often the way of wishes—they fly out of our mouths before we pause to think. That's why I make a distinction between *wishes* and *intentions*. Let's make sure you are setting thoughtful intentions instead of making random wishes!

So how do you figure out how to set an intention without getting a sausage stuck to your nose?

The first step is to quiet your mind.

But now comes the tricky part! Let's say you want a kitten. You get quiet and still. You picture the kitten. It's warm and snuggly. It lays on your belly and purrs. You feel so loved!

It would be easy to stop there, but don't! Picture yourself feeding the kitten and scooping out its litter box. Imagine that your kitten is in a bad mood and scratches you. Now check in with yourself. Do you still feel warm and fuzzy? If so, congratulations, you might truly want a kitten! But if you feel unsure in any way, back up to the point where you felt *so* loved. Maybe what you want is that *feeling*. Perhaps it's not actually about the kitten. If this is the case, instead of setting an intention to get a kitten, you would be wiser to intend that you feel loved.

Let's look at the intention-setting process from another angle (because it's important to try to see around corners and look through walls!). Say that a good friend is having a birthday. You want to make sure it's a very special day. If you set the intention that you will make her a perfect cake, there are a number of things that could go wrong.

* You might *try* to make the perfect cake and learn that baking is way harder than you thought.
* Your definition of a "perfect cake" might be different than hers, like if you love vanilla frosting but she prefers strawberry.
* Maybe she doesn't like cake at all!

What's the solution to this problem?

Instead of intending *specific* things, you might instead simply intend that your friend has an awesome birthday. That leaves many avenues for success! Magic likes a little wiggle room.

So, the first step is to get quiet, and the next step is to think about what you *really* want.

And, now, for the final step:

In traditions in which intentions are set or spells are spoken, a few extra phrases are often added. Popular ones are *and it harm none* or *this or something better*. The first makes it clear to both yourself, and the magic, that whatever you're intending is not so important that hurt should come to anyone in making it come to be. The second acknowledges our limited imagination and leaves space for outcomes even better than what our Nighttime self could dream up. So, at the Night School we use the phrase:

This or something better for all involved.

Once you have an intention thought out and ready to fly, it's time to share it with the Universe—to let your intention be known. This is what we call *casting a spell.*

Casting a spell can be very simple: You can simply speak your intention aloud. But note that many old magics follow the rule of three, meaning you repeat your intention three times. This is a fail-safe, so that if you accidentally shout out in a moment of anger, *You silly woman! I wish that sausage was stuck to your nose!* the magic will simply hold its breath and wait to see if you repeat your request.

Some people add a ritual to their spells as a way of showing the magic a little bit of what they want, as a way of reinforcing the message. For example, if your intention is to have your family travel to the beach this summer, you could lay out a seashell each time you say, *I want us to spend a weekend at the beach!* Spellwork is creative work; there's never just one way to do it. Adding a ritual when you speak your intention is a way of building energy, and putting more *oomph* behind your words.

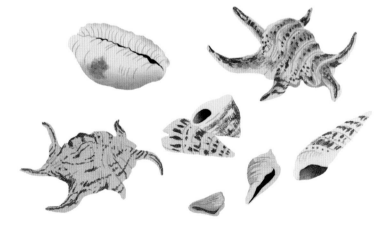

PRACTICE CREATING A RITUAL

Create a ritual around this spell:

I intend to get very good at casting spells!

To create a ritual for this specific spell, break down the words of the spell into separate parts. What represents "being very good" at something? What represents "casting spells?"

Maybe you are excellent at cartwheels, and you want to be as good at spellcasting as you are at cartwheeling! That means the ritual you create could be as simple as saying, *I intend to get very good at casting spells!* And you say this while you are doing a cartwheel . . . or three!

Maybe you believe that magic comes from Mother Earth, and that words on a page represent a spell, so you write the following on a piece of paper: *I intend to get very good at casting spells!* Then you bury it in the earth.

There is no right way to do a ritual, only the way that makes you feel energized!

You might remember that Ms. Marlowe called me a Green Witch. That means that when I do spells, I often use plants from the garden as part of my ritual. For instance, see that vine growing on the stone wall? That's called Boston ivy. When my company, Witchery, throws a party for one of our clients, I use ivy in my pre-party ritual because ivy represents community—it pulls people together! Studying plants for their magical and healing properties is a wonderful way to continue your Night School studies.

The Victorians even had a language of flowers through which they created bouquets that contained coded messages. If you look closer to the ground, in front of the Boston ivy, you'll see marigolds, which the Victorians used to express the sadness of a goodbye and the hope to see the person again. Which is a fine sentiment as we end our time together!

There's just one final thing I'd like you to think about: When I was a student at the Night School, the head teacher used to say, *You can set a spell in motion, but you can't control the timing.* So be patient when you cast a spell. Remember that setting an intention or casting a spell is the first step in a process. Keep the magic alive by remembering your intention each Night. You can repeat it aloud or in your mind. When you do so, *listen* for anything that sounds false or feels incomplete. Don't hesitate to make your spell better as you repeat it! (No need to worry, this doesn't break the rules of magic, because you said *this or something better.*)

There you have it, Night Schoolers! You now know how to set an intention, cast a spell, and create a ritual, and you also know how to set a powerful goal in the daylight world. As you get practiced at spellcasting, you'll find it's useful in both your day and Night lives.

And now we are truly complete! It has been a pleasure teaching you this evening, and do keep Witchery in mind for all your future marketing needs!

Oh dear! Ms. Marlowe seems to have settled down in the valerian patch and fallen asleep. Valerian will do that to you!

I trust you can see yourself home? Picture your Night Spot. Forget the scents of New York City and remember the smells of the place where you live. Hear the Night birds or the traffic patterns that are familiar to you. And when you're ready . . .

Toodle-oo!

field trip NO.5

THE SECRET SECT OF PYTHIAN PRIESTESSES: DIVINE THE PATH OF THE ORACLE

How is it that we're already at our final field trip, Firefly? It's all flown by so fast!

For this last excursion, we'll be meeting the members of the Secret Sect of the Pythian Priestesses. Remember when we visited the Temple of Apollo at Delphi and I told you that was where people from all over the ancient world came to meet with the oracle and hear her predictions? The ancient name for the Oracle of Delphi is the Pythia. And there wasn't just one: There was a whole group of these prophesizing priestesses!

I'm about to let you in on a secret, Firefly: Because these ladies could read the future, they made plans for the continuation of their work. While the Temple of Apollo has long since gone to rubble, the Pythian Priestesses are still prophesizing away, helping folks to know themselves and to make decent decisions for their lives.

YOU'LL NEED:

* ⁎ your journal
* ⁎ a pendulum
* ⁎ a magazine with lots of pictures
* ⁎ a pocket full of pebbles
* ⁎ salt

Grab your compass and face west! Your focal point image is on the next page. Feel a salt-scented breeze on your left cheek and imagine the bitter smell of coffee. And we're off!

Did everyone make it?

Fabulous!

Come right this way. The ladies have prepared their special peppermint hot chocolate. We'll gather around this table in the back so as not to disturb the other customers.

While we wait, let me give you an overview of what you'll be learning this evening! Students are sometimes disappointed that learning the art of divination won't allow them to know with 100 percent certainty who their teacher will be next year or what gift they'll be getting for their birthday.

There is nothing "100 percent certain" about divining, Firefly. Divination is about seeking patterns. It's soft and squishy. It's more like a gummy worm and less like a chocolate bar. It's a very Nighttime activity, focused on the truths of the heart and soul. While your day-self knows that there's only one right answer on a spelling quiz, your Night-self realizes that living is complex and layered—that sometimes life is not as clear-cut as spelling.

And so, divination is a ramble around the twisting paths of time; a pit stop at the crossroads of the cosmos; and, of course, a tea date with the Pythia. It's flying Magic 8 Balls and tarot cards and tea leaves. Divination is a waking dream . . . and a dreaming wake! In other words, divination is 100 percent pure Night. It's untamable, unpredictable, soft and squishy around the edges—and utterly delicious!

Doing divination is also one of the larger lessons you'll learn at the Night School. Because of this, we are doing things a little differently this evening. While we're here on our field trip, you will learn the *steps* of divination. This process can be used whether you are reading tea leaves or tarot cards. The *how-to* lessons for tea leaves, tarot cards, and a number of other things will be delivered to you as handouts once you return home. This will allow you plenty of time to experiment, Firefly! So tonight, you learn the process, and later, on your own time, you get to explore the specifics of different divination practices.

Ah! Here we go! The hot chocolate has arrived and with it, your teacher for the evening.

Since the Pythia tends to speak in riddles, we have a unique arrangement for this class: She sits at my shoulder and whispers what she wants you to know. I do a light-speed translation, then teach the lesson. Brilliant, isn't it? Don't be alarmed if she shifts form. Sometimes she prefers to teach as a white raven. I don't completely understand it, Firefly, and that's okay! Everything needn't be logical.

Hmmm? Oh, yes. She agrees and asks you to put on your Night-goggles and consider everything she's about to teach you through that lens.

Let's begin!

Divination has been around forever, and during those eons, people have used everything from bones and stones to the flight patterns of birds to predict the future. We can't learn all the things tonight (that would take the entirety of the seven-year apprenticeship offered by the Sect of the Pythian Priestesses), so we will focus on a few forms of divination to get you started.

Divination requires the combined skills of close observation and fluid imagining, making it much more art than science. Getting a solid prophecy starts with a crystal-clear question and ends with interpreting the answer you receive.

Here is a step-by-step recipe for cooking up delicious divinations:

1. Observe the patterns.
2. Craft the right question.
3. Choose the type of divination.
4. Create a tabula rasa (don't worry, Firefly, we'll explain this term in a bit).
5. Do the divination.
6. Record the results.
7. Interpret your divination.

We're going to go over these one at a time, and then you'll be ready to jump into divining! Remember, just like any skill, this takes practice. Take your time and some good notes on what works and what doesn't so you can learn from your own experiences!

Okay, here we go!

Step 1:
OBSERVE THE PATTERNS

Let's begin with the much-underrated skill of spotting patterns in the world around you. Your ability to divine relies on prowess in something that may seem sideways to oracle-izing: the art of observing patterns.

Witnessing the cycle of the stars and listening to the ocean's waves reminds us that we're part of something greater, something with its own rhythm. To begin to cultivate an observant way of being, practice walking through your life with your senses open, just like you did when you first visited your Night Spot. Practice this heightened awareness not only during the Night but also throughout the day. Make it your new normal to pay attention to the sighs of the wind, the flight paths of the birds, and the whispers of the leaves. They all have a story to tell if you're willing to listen. Do you live in a city? Not a problem! You still have birds, and trees, and stars. You also have the patterns of people, which can be just as fascinating. Observe how they stand on subway platforms or in line to get coffee. Once you start truly seeing, you'll realize there are patterns everywhere.

Pay attention to the things that are drawing your attention.

That seems obvious, doesn't it, Firefly? But in our busy lives we often make and discard observations faster than a dog sheds hair. Try to slow down and fully notice what you're noticing! Observe the usual patterns and the unusual occurrences, notice things that may be signs or symbols, think about how you feel or what you think when you see a certain image, then try to step outside your thoughts and feelings and back into a place of observation.

Sketch Your Surroundings

Sketching can get your brain to shift gears from judging and making meaning into simply noticing. Attempt to draw either the room you are sitting in or an object within that space. For instance, you could doodle the dimensions of your comfy armchair or sketch the plant in the corner. Try to capture the exact drape and fold of your lap blanket (which will be difficult unless you're an expert drawer, Firefly, but try anyway because it will make you focus in on details).

The act of close observation that occurs when you put pen or pencil to paper is what matters, Firefly, not the final drawing (you can throw your sketch away as soon as you're done). Beginning to notice this level of detail will help you decipher the nuances of your visions, dreams, and divinations.

Step 2:
CRAFT THE RIGHT QUESTION

The question begins the divination process. If there is no question, then the information you get from a divination could be about anything. Let's say you pull a card from your tarot deck. The card is the Tower, which symbolizes endings and destruction. If you didn't ask a question, you'll have no idea what's about to be destroyed: The spider that was about to crawl over your foot? The pizza you forgot you put in the oven for dinner? Or is it a more important warning? If you didn't ask a question before you pulled the card, there's no way to know. So the first step is coming up with a question.

But not all questions are created equal!

Compare these two queries:

> *What should I do next?*

versus

> *Should I join the swim team?*

The first sentence is not very specific, is it? Now compare these two questions:

> *Should I join the swim team?*

versus

> *Will I be happy if I join the swim team?*

The quality of the question determines the quality of the answer. Do you want to know if you'll feel fit and strong? If you will be you happy? If your team will win competitions?

It's easy to imagine a situation where you join the swim team and are winning competitions but don't feel total happiness. It's also easy to envision the opposite: You're not very good at swimming, but you have fun with your swim team friends and love going to practice.

Think about what *exactly* you want to know. Do you want to know if you'll win races or laugh so much your face hurts?

Once you have your well-thought-out question, write it at the top of a fresh journal page before you begin the divining process.

Practice Crafting a Question

Write down the first question that comes to your mind. Don't overthink it.

Now edit that question to make it more specific.

Finally, look at your edit and ask yourself if it's detailed enough. Think about what you really want to know and edit one more time!

Step 3:
CHOOSE THE TYPE OF DIVINATION

We're at step 3, Firefly: *Choose the best type of divination to answer your question.* Let's figure out which of the prophetic pickings is just right for you.

Obviously, to do that, you need to know what your options are. You'll be getting these as a handout, delivered after tonight's class. There are many types of divination, so the Pythian Priestesses have chosen the best ones for beginners! As you read about each option, think about what you might like to try first. Eventually, you can try them all! You might be surprised at which work best for you.

Step 4:
CREATE A TABULA RASA

You're getting very close to having all the knowledge you need to cast your divination, Firefly! We're at the final step before the big moment. Once you have your question ready and have chosen your type of divination, you'll want to clear your mind and energy field so that you can see clearly. The Pythian Priestesses call this creating a tabula rasa.

A tabula rasa was the ancient Roman equivalent of a blank notepad. Instead of being made of paper, it was made of wax. The wax was "blanked" by heating it and then smoothing it out. The same tablet could then be used over and over. A tabula rasa is like a new moon Night: an inky void, full of nothing but possibility.

This is much like removing the smudges from the telescope lens (remember that metaphor from Mystery School, Firefly?). By creating a tabula rasa, you're preparing yourself to receive messages clearly.

There are many ways to "blank" your mind, and over time you'll develop your own rituals. The Pythia recommends three ways to begin. After you read them and check for needed ingredients, choose one to try.

Breathe and Visualize

This is your do-anywhere method for getting yourself clean, clear, and ready to work.

Get comfortable in a seated position, making sure your spine is relatively straight (so the air can move in and out of your lungs easily). Breathe slowly into your belly, imagining the air moving down your spine. Gently release your breath.

On your next breath, picture breathing in the stillness of a new moon Night. Inhale the velvet darkness, letting it soothe your troubles and worries. Breathe out jumbles of words, stray thoughts, and sticky feelings (both your own and anyone else's you may be carrying around with you).

Keep going, pulling clarity and quiet in through your lungs, exhaling everything that doesn't belong to you and your energy body, until all that remains is a tabula rasa ready to receive a divination.

Salt It Out!

In common use and also in divination, salt is prized for its ability to pull out water from other substances (and water is a metaphor for emotions). Salt draws moisture from the interior to the surface. You'll find it used in the kitchen to "salt out" meats and veggies. If you've eaten beef jerky, you've had a food that's been salted out.

Soaking in a tub of salt water will pull out your own emotions so you can release them, and it will "salt out" energies that aren't yours so you can send them down the drain. To do this, fill the bathtub with warm to hot water (test with the tip of your elbow first to make sure your skin doesn't get burned!), add a cup of either sea salt or mineral salt, dim the lights, and let the combination of the salt and heat do their work!

While a soak can be delightful, taking a bath every time you want to use your pendulum is going to get old fast! Instead, try washing your hands using salt as a scrub. Imagine everything that will cloud your intuition washing down the drain!

(Personally, I love salt, Firefly. Those little salt packets at restaurants make a quick cleanse easy when I'm away from home.)

Shake, Rattle, and Roll

Vibration will dislodge even the most stubborn **metaphysical** muck! If dancing it out is your preferred method of relieving stress, grab a rattle and give your aura a rinse at the same time.

No rattle? No problem.

Dried beans, rice, or paper clips in a closed mason jar will do the trick just fine. Rattle all around yourself as you move your body. If something feels like it needs an extra shake or two, trust the sensation. You can add a visualization by imagining anything stuck to you vibrating right off. You'll have a fresh tabula rasa in no time!

Step 5:
DO THE DIVINATION

We're giving you a step-by-step guide to follow every time you do a divination, Firefly. You are now at step 5: *Do the divination.* This is where you'll insert a divination technique and take it for a test drive! But don't do a divination right now! Instead, finish learning all the steps so you have the big picture of how this works.

Step 6:
RECORD THE RESULTS

Take some notes on your divination process and the results!

Yep, it's that simple. . . . Unless you're recording dreams or visions. In that case, follow the more specific instructions provided in the handouts you'll receive later.

Step 7:
INTERPRET YOUR RESULTS

For divinations that come to you with images and symbols, interpretation is as important as the original divining. But since it's your Night-brain doing this work, Firefly, you might find yourself making sideways associations. For instance, now that the Pythia is sitting on my shoulder in her raven form, you might suddenly be thinking about the penguins you saw at the zoo. It doesn't matter that the Pythia is not a penguin: Her bird form made you *think* of a penguin. And that's a form of interpretation.

Not only is it okay to follow these free associations when you have them, but it's necessary when interpreting divinations to pull on different threads and see where they lead. When you are interpreting a divination, you'll want to look at:

1. Where your brain goes when you let it free-associate.
2. What the symbols and images in your divination mean in mythology, folklore, and stories. You'll find this by doing a search at the library or on the internet (with a parent's help, if necessary): *What does a raven symbolize? What does a penguin symbolize?*

And then add the special sauce, Firefly:

3. Ask: What does the symbol mean *to you*? If your grandma had a crow or a raven that she fed sunflower seeds to, and it visited her every morning, a crow or a raven might make you think of your grandma. But it wouldn't make other Night Schoolers think of *their* grandmas (unless everyone's grandma feeds the crows!). You can use an internet search or symbol dictionary as a starting point, but, ultimately, your personal history needs to be added to help you make sense of your divinations.

RESEARCH A SYMBOL AND THINK ABOUT WHAT IT MEANS TO YOU

Choose a symbol you might see on an oracle card or in a dream. It might be something like a butterfly or a doorway. It could also be a color, like blue (each color is thought to have its own meaning, Firefly). Research this symbol's meaning across multiple cultures. Head to your computer, open a web browser, and try typing in the symbol plus the name of a culture (like *butterfly Celtic, butterfly Cherokee, butterfly Egyptian, butterfly Korean*).

First, notice whether your chosen symbol appears in a lot of myths and stories, or only in a few.

Next, compare how your symbol is used across cultures. Can you see the universal traits for your symbol (meaning, does your symbol stand for the same thing in many different cultures?), or does it mean very different things across the world and history?

Now think about why you chose this symbol. What does it mean in your life and experience?

As we finish up this evening, the Pythia has asked me to remind you of one very important thing:

YOU are magic.

If you *ever* forget this, just step into the Night.

The remnants of my hot chocolate are staining the bottom of my mug. They look like a cat . . . no wait, maybe that's a pizza? Oh! I know what it is. It's your Night Spot!

Pull out your compass, Firefly. Face yourself north. Remember the sounds and scents of your own home. Picture it first, then away you go!

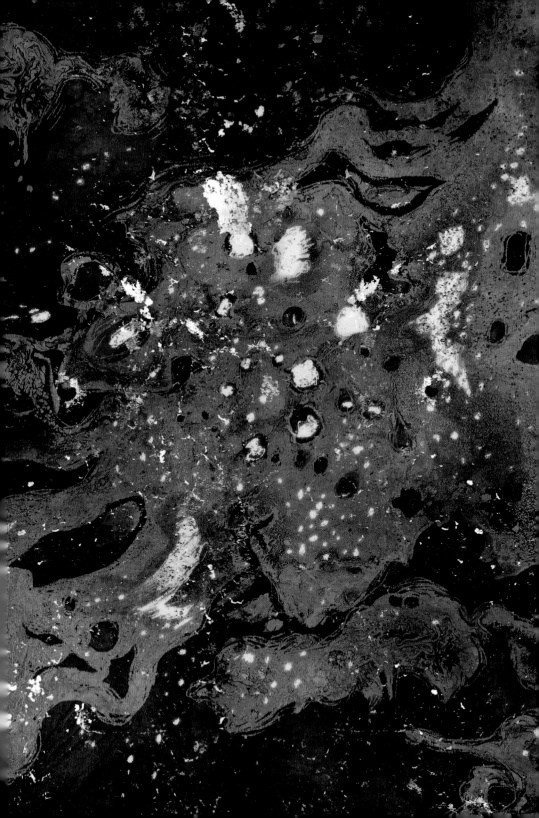

DIVINATION HANDOUTS
for
Night School
STUDENTS

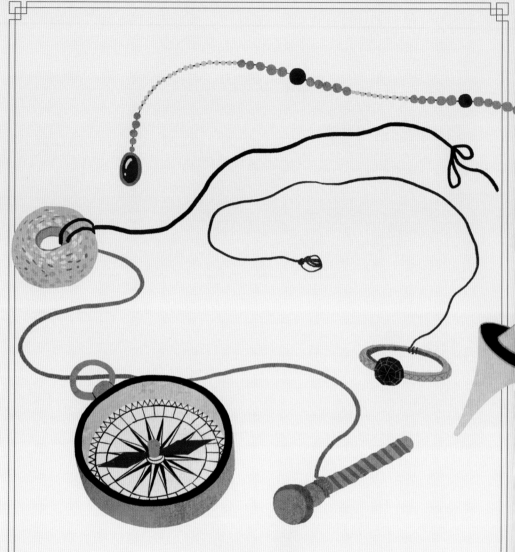

divination option
NO.1

THE PENDULUM

A pendulum is a way of amplifying your Clair—which you learned about in Mystery School, Firefly, on page 52. Your intuition is constantly collecting information. The pendulum gives you access to that info.

If you want to know more about the history of using pendulums, research *dowsing*. Also know that pendulums work well for yes and no questions or to find something on a map.

You can use a pendulum designed specifically for divining or simply use any small bob you can hang on a string or chain (a bob can be a button on a thread, a key on a cord, or a bolt on a piece of twine). A necklace with a charm can work beautifully. If your compass has a loop, you can use that!

Thread the string or chain through the bob and hold both ends so you don't have a knot on top of the bob affecting the balance.

Hold the string so the pendulum swings freely. Some people sit with their elbow balanced on their leg and allow the pendulum to swing between their knees. I hold the pendulum in my right hand and let it swing over my left hand. Try some different positions and see what's comfortable for you, Firefly.

Begin your session by asking the pendulum to show you *yes*. It may swing clockwise, counterclockwise, or back and forth.

Then ask your pendulum to show you *no*. Notice the difference between a *yes* and a *no*. For some people, the pendulum doesn't move at all when the answer is no.

Now you're ready to ask your question and record your results!

Note if your pendulum makes any movements other than the *yes* or *no* that you established. Track those movements over time and see if they are indicating that the outcome of your question doesn't matter or that you're not asking a particularly good question.

Also notice the **velocity** of the swing. My pendulum sometimes feels like the Earth orbiting the sun, gaining a certain gravity and zest in a way that I interpret as "yes, Yes, YES!"

Additionally, you can use your pendulum over a map or a picture of your home to help you locate lost objects. Here's how to do it: Sketch a picture of your home. If doesn't have to be a good picture, but you will want to be able to see things like different rooms, how many floors are in your house, and the like. Hold your pendulum over your picture. Ask the pendulum, "Is my missing shoe here?" as you move your pendulum over the drawing. When you get a *yes*, go to that area of your home and start searching!

You can also use pictures to ask more complex questions than *yes* or *no*. For instance, if you were choosing between two puppies, you could hold your pendulum over a photo of each to get a positive or negative impression.

divination
option
NO. 2

FREE WRITING

If a pendulum doesn't sound like it's quite your speed, try free writing. Sometimes simply asking yourself the question will get you the answer you need.

The process couldn't be easier, Firefly. Just follow these steps:

* Grab your notebook, turn to a blank page, and write your well-thought-out question at the top.
* Set a timer for ten minutes.
* Take a few deep breaths of the Night air and let your eyes go soft, like they do when you're connecting with the Night.
* Then start writing and don't stop for ten minutes.

I can guarantee that you will feel silly or lost or confused for at least the first three minutes. You'll feel like you are making things up, or that you don't know what to write.

Keep writing even if the words don't seem to make sense. Just write anything that comes to your mind (including "I don't know what to write! This is pointless!"). At a certain point your day-brain will step aside and your Night-brain will take over. This is when the magic happens!

If you want to connect with a plant, animal, or crystal, you can ask it what it wants to share, and then let your hand flow across the page. Just *pretend* you know the answer and start writing. Don't worry about making sense of your words: Write first, interpret later! (Need a refresher on inter-pretation? Flip back to page 81.)

divination
option
NO.**3**

ONEIROMANCY

Next up: oneiromancy! *Oneiromancy* is a fancy word for using dreams as a method of divination. It goes back and back and back: In 3000 BCE the Mesopotamian kings were minding (and mining!) their dreams. And a few thousand years later a Greco-Roman dream book called the *Oneirocritica* showed people that dream work was still alive and well. Another thousand years later, the Japanese writer Sei Shōnagon waded through her dreams in *The Pillow Book*. Oneiromancy and the desire to explore the dreamscape seems to be universal.

The setup for oneiromancy is simple, but don't let that fool you. Dreams are slippery, and learning to catch them with your bare hands takes practice and persistence.

Here's your deceptively simple setup for dream divination:

* ✻ Place your journal and a pen on your nightstand within easy reach of you.

* ✻ Before going to sleep, sit on the edge of your bed. Take a few deep breaths with your feet flat on the floor. Set your question in your mind with the intention that you will dream on it and remember your dream.

* ✻ When you wake up, stay very still so you don't scare away your dream.

* ✻ Replay what you remember of your dream while your eyes are still closed, moving the dream from image to words in your mind.

* ✻ When you feel like you've caught it, reach for your journal. Try to keep your movements very small. Don't even turn on the light.

* ✻ Begin writing, listing big ideas and images first so you don't lose them. Then go back and write the dream as a story. Use the first-person present tense (*I am walking through a moonlit garden* instead of *I walked through a moonlit garden*), which is a trick to help you recall more details!

This is the first step. The next step is interpretation, which the Pythian Priestesses talked to you about on page 81. Remember, interpreting is just as important as dreaming!

Record your dreams for a few weeks and see what comes to you. If you're having trouble remembering your dreams, mugwort is a traditional dream aid. The tea isn't tasty, but try three sips before bed or put some of the dried herb in a pouch under your pillow. (Of course, always ask a parent or adult if it's okay for you to drink any herbal teas.)

divination
option
NO.4

DIVINING WITH IMAGES

Tarot and oracle cards (as well as using photos or illustrations from magazines or books) are a way of divining with images, Firefly. Both tarot and oracle cards originate from those used for games in various parts of Europe. In fact, fortune-telling itself was considered a wonderful game centuries ago! Read on, and I'll give you a little history for each of these forms of divination.

Tarot decks have been around for a long time and were first used for a game called *tarocchi*. The oldest surviving tarot set, known as the Visconti-Sforza deck, was created for the Duke of Milan's family around 1440. Milan is in Italy, Firefly. And the images on this set of cards were inspired by popular Carnival costumes. It wasn't until the eighteenth century that the tarot deck became popular as a divination tool, and in modern days, tarot cards are still used for divination.

Tarot decks are based on the suits found in a deck of traditional playing cards. In the tarot deck, those suits relate to the four elements, which we discussed way back at the beginning of the Night School on page 4. Like a cake, tarot cards have layers of meaning and use a complex system of symbolism. While learning all about tarot is more than we can do tonight, if this feels exciting to you, Firefly, you might want to spend time diving into the mysteries of the tarot deck! There are books specifically about tarot to get you started (see the resource section at the end of this book).

Another kind of deck, called an oracle deck, is also used in divination. Oracle decks are thought to have started with a famed French fortune-teller named Marie Anne Adelaide Lenormand (1772–1843). Marie used playing card decks to do cartomancy (that's reading the cards, Firefly).

Often, she would combine a French deck that had four suits—hearts, clubs, diamonds, and spades—with a German gaming deck that had different suits—hearts, acorns, bells, and leaves. These two decks together gave her plenty of symbols to work with. After her death, two decks of cards were published bearing her name: Grand jeu de Mlle Lenormand and Petit Lenormand. These cards are the first of what we now call oracle cards. These decks both had a series of symbols on each card so they could be used for fortune-telling.

Unlike tarot cards, oracle cards are not part of a larger system. In fact, they are much simpler. Each card has one meaning, and they are not necessarily related to the rest of the cards in the deck. In modern oracle decks, each card's meaning is spelled out in a tiny booklet that comes with the deck.

> Both tarot and oracle cards can be used simply for their images, which is how we use them at the Night School. Oracle cards are well suited for exactly the way we do divination at the Night School.

Using either tarot or oracle cards will help your mind somersault into what we call *free association*. Free association is when you set logic aside and let your imagination out to play. When you're feeling unclear or unsure, cards offer your mind a way of coming up with other ways of thinking about your situation. For example, if you're angry at your best friend and you don't know what to do about it, you could draw a card. Your question might be *What should I do about the anger I feel toward my friend?* Say you pull a card with a horse on it. Your first thought might be *My friend is sleek and graceful just like that horse. Sometimes I feel like I'm not good enough when I'm around that person.*

Whoa!

Did you know you had that thought floating in your head?

How does that thought relate to your anger?

Remember, Firefly, divination is not direct. Instead it is soft and slippery. It gives you things to think about instead of exact answers. But realizing that you have many feelings about your friend gives you new ways to think about your anger, which will help you figure out what to do next.

Having a deck and pulling cards is kind of like having a good friend or therapist who asks questions that get you thinking in a whole new way. The images and the words offered by the small booklet that comes with the oracle cards can help you slip the confines of your day-brain.

How to divine with images:

* As always, it starts with your question. Wait until your question has crystallized and feels clear to you, then write it in your notebook.

* When your question is ready, hold your deck (or book, or pile of images) with the back side up between your hands. Breathe in and out, grounding your body and mind in the moment, then imagine your question infusing your hands, bathing the cards in the energy of your query.

* It's now time to draw a card. There are many ways to do this: You can cut the deck and draw a card off the top; you can spread the cards (back side up) and draw whichever feels right; or you can think of a number and count the cards until you get to your number of choice.

* After you draw your card, you'll move into the interpretation phase of the divination. Everything you're seeing in the card and reading in the small booklet relates to your question in some way.

* When interpreting an image, begin by examining the image in detail. Notice the colors and whether the image shows movement or stillness. Identify the natural elements (Earth,

Water, Fire, Air) and how they are represented. Begin noting your observations in your journal, simply writing exactly what you see: *I see a woman in a green dress. She looks sad. Actually, she looks like she's trying to pretend she's happy, but I'm not buying it.* That kind of thing.

∗ Now let your mind free-associate, or just sort of go where it wants, putting all the pieces of your thinking together. For the example above, you might think: *Green is the color of envy. The woman is pretending not to feel what she is really feeling. Is she feeling envy?* Then apply this to your situation and question: *Hmmm, am I pretending a feeling I don't actually feel? Am I envious of someone or something?*

What if you don't have a tarot or oracle deck? No problem! The lovely thing about how we use the cards at the Night School is that they're easily replaced by other sources of imagery, like the illustrations on the pages of a book or photos you've cut from a magazine or printed from your computer. You can also use a book for divination. This is called *bibliomancy,* and it's very simple to do. At the point in the instructions above where you would draw a random card, instead open an illustrated book to a random page.

divination
option
NO.5

READING THE STICKS . . .
OR STONES . . . OR COFFEE GROUNDS!

There is a principle in ancient philosophy that states: *As above, so below.* What this means, Firefly, is that small things follow the same patterns as big things. If you understand this principle, you won't be surprised when I tell you that the pattern of our galaxy, which you can see through a telescope, is very much like the pattern of a cell that you look at under a microscope!

Because of the principle of *as above, so below*, you can analyze the patterns of small things like tea leaves, or sticks, or stones, or even coffee grounds to get a feel for the larger patterns at play. When you use techniques like tasseography (that's a fancy word for reading tea leaves or coffee grounds) or lithomancy (reading stones), you're looking for patterns and shapes. These shapes can be used to tell a story about the question you're asking or they may be a trigger for your intuition and help you come to an answer.

For instance, let's say you are wondering how much you need to study for an upcoming test at school. You shake up a handful of pebbles and throw them down. Oddly, they seem to form the shape of your dog's head, complete with his funny little ears. As you look at the pattern of the pebbles you suddenly think, *I've studied hard already. I've got this! I'm going to take Pluto for a walk instead of studying more.* And voilà! You have just used lithomancy!

As usual, you must begin with a well-crafted question. Your exact next step to answering the question is going to depend on what you've chosen for your reading. Sticks and stones are usually shaken and thrown. These are fine tools if you are reading for yourself. With tea leaves and coffee grounds, the tea or coffee is sipped and the leaves or grounds left at the bottom of the cup are what's read. That's how the Pythian Priestesses do it at Sacred Grounds, Firefly. People finish their coffee, and when their server comes to take the mug away, she might casually say, "Oh look! You have a four-leaf-clover pattern in the grounds at the bottom of your cup. I think it's going to be a lucky day!" The priestesses are so good, I bet they could even manage a divination with the cocoa left at the bottom of your hot chocolate mug!

Over the long history of divination, people have read everything from oil to flour to ink stains, so don't feel limited to the exact things I mentioned before. You can ask your question and scatter rice, beans, or spaghetti sticks from your kitchen if you so desire. (I'd recommend doing so on a plate, Firefly, so you don't waste food.) It's the asking of the question, and your intention to find the pattern within the answer, that is the important part, not the exact tool used.

After you cast the divination, the next step is to soften your gaze and look for patterns.

Interpretation of these patterns is a chance to exercise your intuition: Observe, then write down what you see, think, and feel. Remember, Firefly, you're using your Night-brain, allowing things to flow and connect freely.

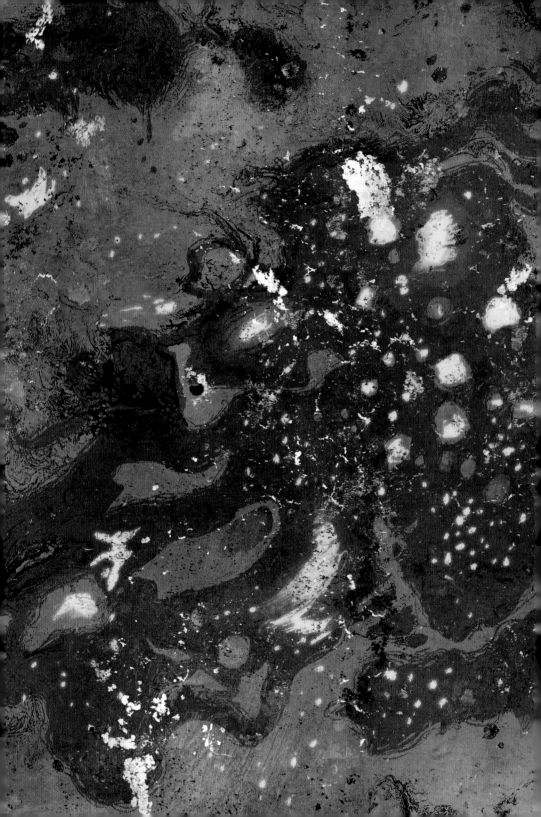

TEST YOURSELF!

It's a wrap, Firefly! Thanks for traveling the Night with me.

It's test time! Let's see what you've learned. Take out your notebook and answer the following questions.

 * What is magic, and where is it found?
 * What are the four elements, and why do they matter?
 * Do we live in a world where everything stays the same always?
 * Why is it important to know yourself?
 * What's the difference between setting an intention and making a wish?
 * What are the Clairs, and which is yours?
 * Does divination have all the answers?
 * Bonus question: Recite the Night School mantra!

I'm sure you did fantastically on your exam, Firefly! You've been an excellent student. I was most impressed with your visualization skills—that was some flawless traveling you did.

And now, I must be off. The Guild of Modern Alchemy has asked me to come lecture on how to turn dragon's gold into moonstones. No doubt, I will see you again in the Night!

Yours in starlight,

Bea Marlowe

Head teacher, the Night School

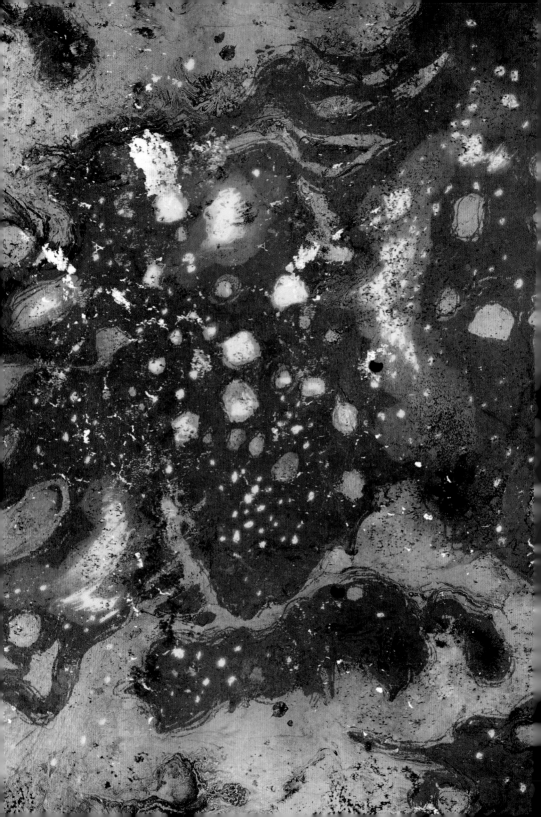

Night Words:
A Glossary of Unfamiliar Terms

alchemy: This was the earliest form of chemistry. While alchemists are known for trying to discover how to make metals into gold, how to cure all diseases, and how to live forever, they also did more everyday science. Alchemy was popular during the medieval era (between 470 and 1400 CE, Firefly), before the invention of modern chemistry.

amphitheater: A building placed out in the open and in the shape of an oval or a circle with different levels of seating. Amphitheaters were very common in Ancient Rome, where contests or various forms of live entertainment were held for the public to watch.

astrologer: A person who studies the stars and planets and how these celestial bodies influence or dictate what happens to people as well as to the Earth.

aura: A sort of area of energy surrounding a person or living creature. This is something you might feel coming off of someone you walk near or are close to, Firefly.

cauldron: A fancy word for a large pot or kettle that is mainly used to boil liquids.

mantra: A way of calling upon something mystical, such as a spell, a magical ritual, or even a simple string of words used to meditate or create a larger meaning around an event or in a certain setting. The repetition of words or short phrases is key to a mantra and is used to help you better focus, especially during meditation.

metaphor: This is a figure of speech, Firefly, that helps someone understand how something is like (or similar to) something else. When using a metaphor, a person will take one thing and substitute it for another thing to show how they are similar.

metaphysical: This is a tricky concept to get, but basically this means something is a part of or related to something else that is beyond our five senses but that does exist. This might be something supernatural (which we cannot see in our Universe but that is believed to exist) or something outside of what we perceive that cannot actually be proven to be there. The word *meta* is from the Greek, meaning "beyond." So *metaphysical* means "beyond the physical."

philosophy: The systematic study of fundamental questions about the nature of knowledge, reality, and existence. The word *philosophy* comes from the ancient Greek and means "love of wisdom." The four branches of philosophy are the study of knowledge, the study of reality, the study of ethics, and the study of logic.

portico: Usually found in ancient or classical buildings, this is the part you might find at the entrance of a building or temple, above a number of columns that hold up the building's roof.

Pythian: Associated with the oracle of Apollo or with Delphi, where the oracle was said to reside.

ritual: A ceremony that uses symbolism to turn thoughts into action, often in a repeated way. For example, each time you think of gathering all your friends, you could walk in a circle.

spirituality: This is a way of being that is usually related to something sacred or supernatural. There are many forms of spirituality, Firefly, and many ways to express this in oneself.

velocity: The speed that something moves.

visualization: The process or way of seeing something in your mind and making it feel almost real. This is also often called making a "mental image."

watch fob: A short strap, chain, or other item that attaches to a watch piece and that allows the watch to hang. Think of an old-timey image of an elderly gentleman checking the time by pulling a watch out of his pocket by a chain, and that's what a watch fob is, Firefly.

Resources for Night School Graduates (and Their Adults)

Dream On: A Kid's Guide to Interpreting Dreams by Cerridwen Greenleaf, illustrated by Khoa Le

How to Speak Flower: A Kid's Guide to Buds, Blooms, and Blossoms by Molly Williams, illustrated by Miriam Bos

The Junior Astrologer's Handbook: A Kid's Guide to Astrological Signs, the Zodiac, and More by Nikki Van De Car, illustrated by Uta Krogmann

The Junior Witch's Handbook: A Kid's Guide to White Magic, Spells, and Rituals by Nikki Van De Car, illustrated by Uta Krogmann

The Junior Tarot Reader's Handbook: A Kid's Guide to Reading Cards by Nikki Van De Car, illustrated by Uta Krogmann

Practical Magic for Kids: Your Guide to Crystals, Horoscopes, Dreams, and More by Nikki Van De Car, illustrated by Katie Vernon

Card decks for divining with images:

The Illustrated Bestiary Oracle Cards: 36-Card Deck of Inspiring Animals by Maia Toll

The Junior Astrologer's Oracle Deck and Guidebook: 44 Cards for Budding Mystics by Nikki Van De Car, illustrated by Uta Krogmann

The Junior Tarot Reader's Deck and Guidebook: 78 Cards for Budding Mystics by Nikki Van De Car, illustrated by Uta Krogmann

For the adults in your life who want their own magical coursework:

The Night School: Lessons in Moonlight, Magic, and the Mysteries of Being Human by Maia Toll, illustrated by Lucille Clerc

The Illustrated Herbiary: Guidance and Rituals from 36 Bewitching Botanicals by Maia Toll

The Illustrated Beastiary: Guidance and Rituals from 36 Inspiring Animals by Maia Toll

The Illustrated Crystallary: Guidance and Rituals for 36 Magical Gems and Minerals by Maia Toll

The Wild Wisdom Companion: A Guided Journey into the Mystical Rhythms of the Natural World, Season by Season by Maia Toll

Acknowledgments

When I got the email telling me the team at Running Press wanted me to adapt *The Night School* into a book for younger mystics, I ran outside, danced in a circle, and shouted *YES!* to the treetops. (Then calmly went back in the house and typed a more reasonable reply!) Getting to spend extra time in the world of Bea Marlowe and thinking about how to explain magic to one of my favorite age groups has been an absolute joy. Thanks to my agent—Laura Lee Mattingly—for making this happen.

So much gratitude to the RP team: Melanie Gold, Frances J. Soo Ping Chow, Becca Matheson, Kara Thornton, and Elizabeth Parks. Special thanks to my editor Julie Matysik, for being an exceptional partner in this re-creation process, and to Khoa Le for bringing my words to life.

Thanks to my four-legged friends Nyssa, Finn, and Winnie for keeping me company during the writing process (extra biscuits all around!) and to Andrew for bringing home pizzas so I didn't have to worry about dinner.

Special thanks to my past elementary school students. I imagine you all as I type, looking to see what makes you stop to think and what makes you laugh. I know you are all grown up now, but I hold your younger selves in my heart.

About the Author and Illustrator

Maia Toll is the author of the award-winning Wild Wisdom series, including *The Illustrated Herbiary*, and of *The Night School* and *Letting Magic In*. After pursuing an undergraduate degree in philosophy at the University of Michigan and a master's at New York University, Toll taught both second and fourth grades. A sabbatical from teaching found her apprenticed to a traditional healer in Ireland, where she studied the alchemy of medicine making and the psycho-spiritual aspects of healing that ultimately became a new calling. She is the co-owner of the retail store Herbiary, with locations in Asheville, North Carolina, and Philadelphia, Pennsylvania. You can find her online at maiatoll.com.

Based in Ho Chi Minh City, Vietnam, **Khoa Le** is the author and illustrator of numerous picture books. Alongside Khoa's passion for reading, art, and music, she draws inspiration from her travels, where she discovers the beauty of the world—and the magic within it. Khoa finds solace in her small studio, accompanied by her beloved cats, and also cherishes profound tranquility in nature.